Exceptional Board Practices

THE SOURCE in ACTION

Library of Congress Cataloging-in-Publication Data

Exceptional board practices : the source in action.

p. cm.

ISBN 1-58686-099-2 (pbk.)

1. Boards of directors. 2. Nonprofit organizations--Management. 3. Corporate governance. I. BoardSource (Organization)

HD2745.E93 2007

658.4'22--dc22

2007027260

© 2008 BoardSource.
First printing, October 2007.
ISBN 1-58686-099-2

Published by BoardSource
1828 L Street, NW, Suite 900
Washington, DC 20036

Exceptional Board Practices: The Source in Action
This publication may not be reproduced without permission. Permission can be obtained by completing a request for permission form located at www.boardsource.org. Revenue from publications sales ensures the capacity of BoardSource to produce resources and provide services to strengthen the governing boards of nonprofit organizations. Copies of this book and all other BoardSource publications can be ordered by calling 800-883-6262. Discounts are available for bulk purchases.

The views in each BoardSource publication are those of its authors, and do not represent official positions of BoardSource or its sponsoring organizations. Information and guidance in this book is provided with the understanding that BoardSource is not engaged in rendering professional opinions. If such opinions are required, the services of an attorney should be sought.

Formerly the National Center for Nonprofit Boards

BoardSource, formerly the National Center for Nonprofit Boards, is the premier resource for practical information, tools and best practices, training, and leadership development for board members of nonprofit organizations worldwide. Through our highly acclaimed programs and services, BoardSource enables organizations to fulfill their missions by helping build strong and effective nonprofit boards.

BoardSource provides assistance and resources to nonprofit leaders through workshops, training, and our extensive Web site, www.boardsource.org. A team of BoardSource governance consultants works directly with nonprofit leaders to design specialized solutions to meet organizations' needs and assists nongovernmental organizations around the world through partnerships and capacity building. As the world's largest, most comprehensive publisher of materials on nonprofit governance, BoardSource offers a wide selection of books, videotapes, CDs, and online tools. BoardSource also hosts the BoardSource Leadership Forum, bringing together governance experts, board members, and chief executives of nonprofit organizations from around the world.

Created out of the nonprofit sector's critical need for governance guidance and expertise, BoardSource is a 501(c)(3) nonprofit organization that has provided practical solutions to nonprofit organizations of all sizes in diverse communities. In 2001, BoardSource changed its name from the National Center for Nonprofit Boards to better reflect its mission. Today, BoardSource has approximately 11,000 members and has served more than 75,000 nonprofit leaders.

For more information, please visit our Web site, www.boardsource.org, e-mail us at mail@boardsource.org, or call us at 800-883-6262.

Have You Used These BoardSource Resources?

BOOKS

The Source: Twelve Principles of Governance That Power Exceptional Boards

The Nonprofit Board Answer Book: A Practical Guide for Board Members and Chief Executives, Second Edition

Culture of Inquiry: Healthy Debate in the Boardroom

Getting the Best from Your Board: An Executive's Guide to a Successful Partnership

The Board Chair Handbook, Second Edition

Driving Strategic Planning: A Nonprofit Executive's Guide

Meet Smarter: A Guide to Better Nonprofit Board Meetings

The Board Building Cycle: Nine Steps to Finding, Recruiting, and Engaging Nonprofit Board Members, Second Edition

The Nonprofit Policy Sampler, Second Edition

The Nonprofit Dashboard: A Tool for Tracking Progress

Presenting: Nonprofit Financials

The Nonprofit Legal Landscape

Self-Assessment for Nonprofit Governing Boards

Assessment of the Chief Executive, Revised Edition

Fearless Fundraising

The Nonprofit Board's Guide to Bylaws

Understanding Nonprofit Financial Statements, Second Edition

Transforming Board Structure: Strategies for Committees and Task Forces

THE GOVERNANCE SERIES

1. *Ten Basic Responsibilities of Nonprofit Boards*
2. *Financial Responsibilities of Nonprofit Boards*
3. *Structures and Practices of Nonprofit Boards*
4. *Fundraising Responsibilities of Nonprofit Boards*
5. *Legal Responsibilities of Nonprofit Boards*
6. *The Nonprofit Board's Role in Setting and Advancing the Mission*
7. *The Nonprofit Board's Role in Planning and Evaluation*
8. *How To Help Your Board Govern More and Manage Less*
9. *Leadership Roles in Nonprofit Governance*

For an up-to-date list of publications and information about current prices, membership, and other services, please call BoardSource at 800-883-6262 or visit our Web site at www.boardsource.org.

Table of Contents

Preface viii

Introduction ix

*The Source: Twelve Principles of Governance That Power
Exceptional Boards* xii

Principle 1: Constructive Partnership

    Constructing a Partnership 1
        M. Christine DeVita, The Wallace Foundation

    It's Lonely at the Top 4
        Joshua Mintz, Cavanaugh, Hagan, Pierson & Mintz, Inc.

    Frequently Asked Questions about Executive Compensation 7
        Brian H. Vogel, Quatt Associates, Inc.
        Charles W. Quatt, Quatt Associates, Inc.

    Teamwork That Works 9
        George C. Benson, Michigan State University Foundation
        Edward James, Michigan State University Foundation

Principle 2: Mission Driven

    Living Your Mission: What's Behind the 17 Words? 15
        Keith Timko, Leader to Leader Institute

    Vermont Foodbank Stays True to Its Mission 19
        Deborah A. Flateman, Vermont Foodbank

    Vision and Values 21
        Kay Sprinkel Grace, Transforming Philanthropy, LLC

Principle 3: Strategic Thinking

    Thinking Outside the Boardroom 25
        Terry Williams, McKinsey & Company

    Design for the Future: Creating a Strategic Plan That Works 28
        John DiConsiglio, BoardSource

    Driving Strategic Planning 32
        Deborah L. Kocsis, Cornerstone Consulting Associates, LLC
        Susan A. Waechter, Cornerstone Consulting Associates, LLC

    Changing Our Mindset 36
        Carl Brooks, The Executive Leadership Council

Principle 4: Culture of Inquiry

Curious Boards 41
    Nancy Axelrod, NonProfit Leadership Services

Rattle Your Board 44
    Sandra R. Hughes, BoardSource

A Tradition of Dialogue 46
    Lewis M. Gedansky, Project Management Institute

Principle 5: Independent-Mindedness

Declaration of Independence 51
    Maureen K. Robinson, Consultant

Conflicts of Interest: Avoiding the Bad and Managing the Good 53
    BoardSource White Paper

Daring To Innovate 56
    Lowell Noteboom, The Saint Paul Chamber Orchestra

Principle 6: Ethos of Transparency

Through the Looking Glass 61
    Anne Cohn Donnelly, Northwestern University

Rocking the Cradle 64
    Julie S. Tye, The Cradle

To Disclose or Not To Disclose 66
    BoardSource Topic Paper

Principle 7: Compliance with Integrity

Legal. Ethical. Exceptional. 71
    Margaret L. Ackerley, World Wildlife Fund

Audit Rules 74
    BoardSource White Paper

Beyond Compliance 76
    Trinita Logue, Illinois Facilities Fund

Principle 8: Sustaining Resources

Turning Up the Volume 81
    David H. Hosley, KVIE Public Television

Funding the Future 85
    Jennifer Proga, Deutsche Bank Securities Inc.

Putting Your Money Where Your Mouth Is 89
    Kim Klein, Jossey-Bass

Going Above and Beyond 91
    Jane Mentzinger, Chicago Communities In Schools

Principle 9: Results-Oriented

Are We There Yet? The Board's Role in Evaluating
Mission Achievement 97
   Peter York, TCC Group

Evaluation: A Blend of Art and Science 100
   John DiConsiglio, BoardSource

Measuring Success with a Pyramid 104
   Kathleen Wagner, Philadelphia Zoo

Principle 10: Intentional Board Practices

Good Intentions 109
   Charles F. Dambach, Alliance for Peacebuilding

A Winning Number 112
   Duane A. Brown, American Diabetes Association

Finding Inspiration in Our Own Backyard 114
   Susan Sanow, Center for Nonprofit Advancement

Principle 11: Continuous Learning

Continuous Learning 119
   Melissa Davis, YMCA of the USA

Opportunities To Grow 123
   Janet Murguía, National Council of La Raza

Principle 12: Revitalization

Revitalizing Your Board 129
   Jameson A. Baxter, Baxter Associates, Inc.

Roles and Responsibilities of Board Officers 132
   Barbara Lawrence, Consultant
   Outi Flynn, BoardSource

The Board Member Shortage 134
   John DiConsiglio, BoardSource

Start Kidding Yourself 137
   Donald T. Floyd, National 4-H Council
   Natalie Cheng, National 4-H Council

Preface

With the publication in 2005 of *The Source: Twelve Principles of Governance That Power Exceptional Boards,* BoardSource issued a call-to-action for nonprofit boards: Make a discernable difference in your organization by moving from passive stewardship to active leadership. *Exceptional Board Practices: The Source in Action* is a companion to that "little black book" and seconds our call-to-action.

Targeted to board members, chief executives, and professional staff of the more than 1.6 million nonprofit organizations in the United States, both *The Source: Twelve Principles of Governance That Power Exceptional Boards* and *Exceptional Board Practices: The Source in Action* are designed to help you operate at the highest and best use of your collective ability.

The Source: Twelve Principles of Governance That Power Exceptional Boards reflects the collective wisdom of a remarkable group of experts with decades of board experience. By exploring the characteristics of exceptional boards and defining and analyzing their common traits, this group distilled the essence of what exceptional boards do into 12 principles. Aspirational in nature, these principles describe an empowered board and provide a vision of what is possible.

Yes, possible. Real organizations live the 12 principles. Since the publication of *The Source: Twelve Principles of Governance That Power Exceptional Boards,* BoardSource has showcased some of these organizations in *Board Member*®, our bimonthly member periodical. *Exceptional Board Practices: The Source in Action* is a compilation of these articles, plus pertinent information from our books, topic papers, and white papers.

This book is organized by principle. We begin our exploration of each with a short definition. You'll discover that each principle is quite broad in scope and encompasses a number of exceptional practices. Don't let these definitions intimidate you. We follow them with one or two approachable, actionable "dimensions" that focus your attention on one component of a principle at a time. We then introduce you to real board members, chief executives, staff, and consultants who live or teach the principles. By sharing their insights, experiences, lessons learned, and exceptional practices, they demonstrate how to put the 12 principles into practice.

As you will learn, becoming exceptional is a creative and collaborative process that involves almost everyone associated with your organization. It requires vision, passion, commitment, perseverance, time, and money. It might necessitate a change in mindset, but it can be accomplished. Your board can move from being a responsible board to being an exceptional board that adds significant value to your organization and its advance on mission. *Exceptional Board Practices: The Source in Action* is here to help.

Introduction

Governance matters

The heightened public debate and increased regulatory scrutiny regarding nonprofit governance has largely centered on compliance. With exposés in the press and congressional hearings highlighting malfeasance, it's no wonder that the focus has been on legal and ethical responsibilities. While attention to those concerns is absolutely essential, boards need to do more to help their organizations meet the challenges of their missions.

With more than one million organizations that receive nearly $250 billion in charitable contributions, the size and influence of the nonprofit sector make it imperative that nonprofit boards operate ethically, legally, and to their fullest potential. Failure to carry out this critical role can have significant ramifications, from lost opportunities and mission drift to risky behavior and even bankruptcy.

There's more to good governance than compliance

Governance is not an either/or dilemma. It's a both/and situation — both compliance and leadership, oversight and fundraising, challenge and support. Boards must focus on compliance and on advancing their organization's mission through active leadership.

A board may meet every legal requirement, adhere to proper procedures, and still be ineffective if it is not engaged in setting strategic direction and supporting the organization. If a board neglects the full range of its responsibilities, it may preclude the organization from reaching its potential.

Good governance is about providing critical capital — intellect, reputation, resources, and access — to strengthen the organization and in turn the community it serves. An exceptional board recognizes the impact of its leadership, and board members understand that they must be thoughtful and engaged leaders, not competent but passive stewards.

The source of power

Boards often represent underperforming assets for nonprofit organizations that need every resource they can muster. To help boards operate at the best and highest use of their collective ability, BoardSource developed *The Source: Twelve Principles of Governance That Power Exceptional Boards*. Drawing on observations, academic knowledge, and proven practices, we identified the common traits and actions of boards that have made discernible differences to their organizations.

Those boards that made discernable differences to their organizations behaved differently from other boards. To highlight these differences, we distinguished between "responsible" boards and "exceptional" boards. A responsible board is capable and dutiful in carrying out its responsibilities. This is not always an easy feat, nor should it be taken for granted by either board or staff members. A responsible board understands its fiduciary obligations, and it adds value to the organization by approving strategic plans and budgets, regularly reviewing financial statements, evaluating the chief executive annually, and participating in fundraising.

An exceptional board operates on a higher level that is both "more" and "different." Undoubtedly, its members give more — of their time, talent, and treasure. But, they also give differently — their time may be spent more wisely, their skills and social networks better leveraged, and their treasure more strategically deployed. Exceptional boards measure organizational impact and evaluate their own performance, discuss and debate issues, and open doors and make connections.

The difference between responsible and exceptional lies in thoughtfulness and intentionality, action and engagement, knowledge and communication. This difference is what we call the source of power. Using it has a multiplier effect on board performance.

Common denominators

As Peter Drucker said, "Management is doing things right; leadership is doing the right things." Boards need to add how they govern to that maxim. They need to invest time and energy in building collaborative relationships among board members and with the chief executive. They need to be willing and able to think strategically, challenge ideas, and probe for better solutions. While they must bring independent thinking to decision making, they must do so collegially and with an eye toward inviting consensus. In the give and take in the boardroom, they must remember that governance is, fundamentally, a team sport.

The 12 principles of governance, presented on the following pages, get at what boards do and how they do it. They include the fundamentals, such as financial oversight activities, and the intangibles, such as group dynamics. They depend as much on a good board as on a good chief executive. They share some common denominators that enable the board to operate at an exceptional level.

A frank and open relationship

In order to function at the exceptional level, the chief executive must be more than competent and confident. He or she must also be open and honest with the board. The board, in turn, must be committed to ensuring success, while recognizing that nonprofit organizations are complex and constantly changing. As interlocking pieces in a jigsaw puzzle that together create a complete picture, the chief executive and the board are complements, with mutual trust, respect, and appreciation building the foundation for a leadership team that can handle short- and long-term challenges.

Consider this: Working together, the board and head of an independent school created a leadership succession plan a few years before the head of the school was to retire. Board and staff members participated in a collaborative, holistic review process that included articulating the institution's values, evaluating the school's other internal infrastructure needs, and assessing the board — all before the executive search officially started.

Intentionality

As Cyril Houle said, "A good board is a victory, not a gift." Great governance doesn't just happen by accident. It takes the right people in the right place at the right time. Who's on a board matters, and board composition is an important indicator of an exceptional board. An exceptional board is also thoughtful, self-aware, and proactive. It balances the need for long-term stability with the need to adapt its own structures and practices as circumstances change and the organization evolves.

Consider this: A university foundation board, after asking how it could add real value to the institution, shifted the foundation's focus from fundraising to commercialization of intellectual property. In turn, the board populated itself with individuals who have significant professional expertise in law, finance, and research and development. Given the foundation's new role, the board also redefined its relationship with the university's administration and governing board, as well as with foundation and fundraising staff.

Engagement

Board work is just that, work. It requires more than mere attendance at meetings. It requires of board members personal motivation and commitment, as well as intellectual curiosity and challenge. They must share a passion for the organization's cause. In turn, the chief executive must be ready, willing, and able to engage board members in making sense of situations, in determining what matters, and in solving dilemmas. Neither the board nor the chief executive can simply go through the governance motions and expect great results.

Consider this: A board member led a process that resulted in an emotionally powerful vision statement at an environmental organization. The board and the staff were inspired to reframe strategies, elevate goals, and embark on an ambitious fundraising campaign. The campaign raised significantly more money than expected, fueling even greater conservation success.

Benefits of *The Source*

The 12 principles represent the wisdom of a working group of nine governance experts and insights from an advisory panel of 27 distinguished leaders from across the nonprofit and corporate sectors. These principles are intended to focus the conversation about nonprofit boards on the core issues that we believe make the most difference to board performance and, in turn, to organizational success.

The 12 principles help board members understand and meet the expectations and requirements of their positions, providing a vision of what is possible and a way to reach a higher level of effectiveness. They also serve as a tool for chief executives, offering a vision of an empowered board that is a strategic asset to be leveraged, not an obstacle to be circumvented.

Nonprofit organizations — public charities and private foundations alike — differ in size, structure, and complexity, but the characteristics of exceptional governance do not. These 12 principles are universal. They represent the essence of what great boards do differently and how they do it.

Exceptional nonprofit boards advance the common good through uncommonly good work.

A GLIMPSE OF EXCEPTIONAL BOARDS

A large professional society spent a year identifying what the board had learned from governance changes, where it could add the greatest value, how it could work most effectively with staff, and where it should invest time over the next year. The results were used to orient and assimilate new board members, engage less-active board members, and involve the entire board in changes to policies and practices.

A state-based nonprofit financial institution has a board that's committed to the mission and organization, as evidenced by 100 percent attendance at meetings. Board members are prepared, engaged, and active in committees. Already known for an impeccable organization, outstanding fiduciary oversight and compliance, and transparency, the board now seeks to improve its capabilities in strategic thinking and visioning, and is recruiting accordingly.

Reprinted from Board Member®, *Volume 14, Number 3, June/July 2005.*

The Source: Twelve Principles of Governance That Power Exceptional Boards

Exceptional boards add significant value to their organizations, making a discernible difference in their advance on mission. Good governance requires the board to balance its role as an oversight body with its role as a force supporting the organization. The difference between responsible and exceptional boards lies in thoughtfulness and intentionality, action and engagement, knowledge and communication. The following 12 principles offer chief executives a description of an empowered board that is a strategic asset to be leveraged. They provide board members with a vision of what is possible and a way to add lasting value to the organizations they lead.

CONSTRUCTIVE PARTNERSHIP [1]

Exceptional boards govern in constructive partnership with the chief executive, recognizing that the effectiveness of the board and chief executive are interdependent. They build this partnership through trust, candor, respect, and honest communication.

MISSION DRIVEN [2]

Exceptional boards shape and uphold the mission, articulate a compelling vision, and ensure the congruence between decisions and core values. They treat questions of mission, vision, and core values not as exercises to be done once, but as statements of crucial importance to be drilled down and folded into deliberations.

STRATEGIC THINKING [3]

Exceptional boards allocate time to what matters most and continuously engage in strategic thinking to hone the organization's direction. They not only align agendas and goals with strategic priorities but also use them for assessing the chief executive, driving meeting agendas, and shaping board recruitment.

CULTURE OF INQUIRY [4]

Exceptional boards institutionalize a culture of inquiry, mutual respect, and constructive debate that lead to sound and shared decision making. They seek more information, question assumptions, and challenge conclusions so that they may advocate for solutions based on analysis.

INDEPENDENT-MINDEDNESS [5]

Exceptional boards are independent-minded. They apply rigorous conflict-of-interest procedures, and their board members put the interests of the organization above all else when making decisions. They do not allow their votes to be unduly influenced by loyalty to the chief executive or by seniority, position, or reputation of fellow board members, staff, or donors.

ETHOS OF TRANSPARENCY [6]

Exceptional boards promote an ethos of transparency by ensuring that donors, stakeholders, and interested members of the public have access to appropriate and accurate information regarding finances, operations, and results. They also extend transparency internally, ensuring that every board member has equal access to relevant materials when making decisions.

COMPLIANCE WITH INTEGRITY [7]

Exceptional boards promote strong ethical values and disciplined compliance by establishing appropriate mechanisms for active oversight. They use these mechanisms, such as independent audits, to ensure accountability and sufficient controls; to deepen their understanding of the organization; and to reduce the risk of waste, fraud, and abuse.

SUSTAINING RESOURCES [8]

Exceptional boards link bold visions and ambitious plans to financial support, expertise, and networks of influence. Linking budgeting to strategic planning, they approve activities that can be realistically financed with existing or attainable resources, while ensuring that the organization has the infrastructure and internal capacity it needs.

RESULTS-ORIENTED [9]

Exceptional boards are results-oriented. They measure the organization's progress toward mission and evaluate the performance of major programs and services. They gauge efficiency, effectiveness, and impact, while simultaneously assessing the quality of service delivery, integrating benchmarks against peers, and calculating return on investment.

INTENTIONAL BOARD PRACTICES [10]

Exceptional boards intentionally structure themselves to fulfill essential governance duties and to support organizational priorities. Making governance intentional, not incidental, exceptional boards invest in structures and practices that can be thoughtfully adapted to changing circumstances.

CONTINUOUS LEARNING [11]

Exceptional boards embrace the qualities of a continuous learning organization, evaluating their own performance and assessing the value they add to the organization. They embed learning opportunities into routine governance work and in activities outside of the boardroom.

REVITALIZATION [12]

Exceptional boards energize themselves through planned turnover, thoughtful recruitment, and inclusiveness. They see the correlation between mission, strategy, and board composition, and they understand the importance of fresh perspectives and the risks of closed groups. They revitalize themselves through diversity of experience and through continuous recruitment.

Adapted from The Source: Twelve Principles of Governance That Power Exceptional Boards, *BoardSource, 2005 and reprinted from* Board Member®, *Volume 14, Number 3, June/July 2005.*

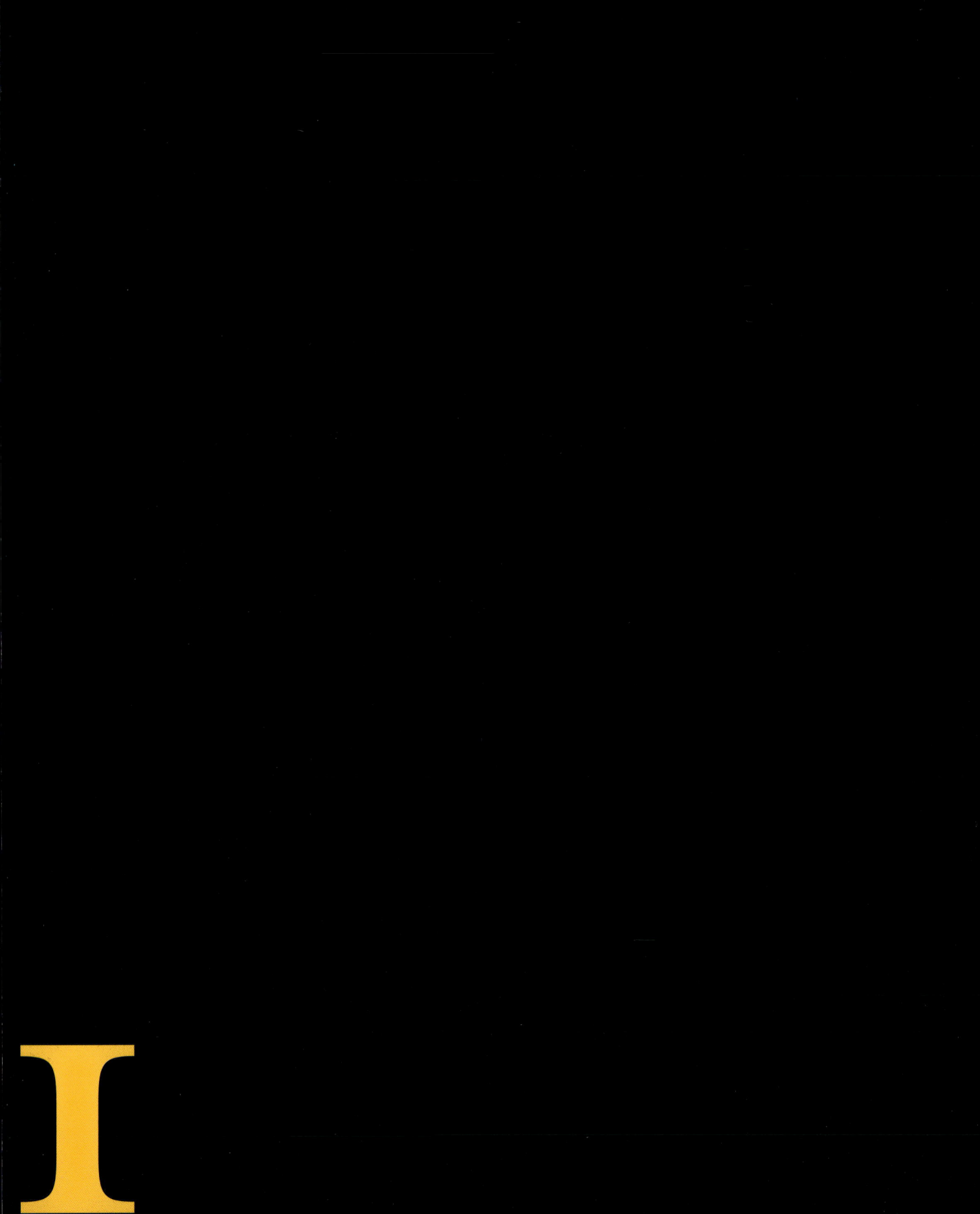

CONSTRUCTIVE PARTNERSHIP I

Exceptional boards govern in constructive partnership with the chief executive, recognizing that the effectiveness of the board and chief executive are interdependent.

DIMENSIONS

- **PARTNERSHIP** Exceptional boards forge a partnership with the chief executive through respect for the distinct roles and responsibilities of each, trust, candor, frequent communication, and support. They encourage the chief executive to pose questions, offer answers, and share bad as well as good news early and openly.

- **SUPERVISION** Exceptional boards evaluate the chief executive's performance annually and encourage the chief executive to strengthen skills when necessary. They set a fair and competitive compensation package for the chief executive, continually evaluate the organization's leadership needs as part of succession planning, and, when it is in the best interests of the organization, undertake the difficult task of replacing the chief executive.

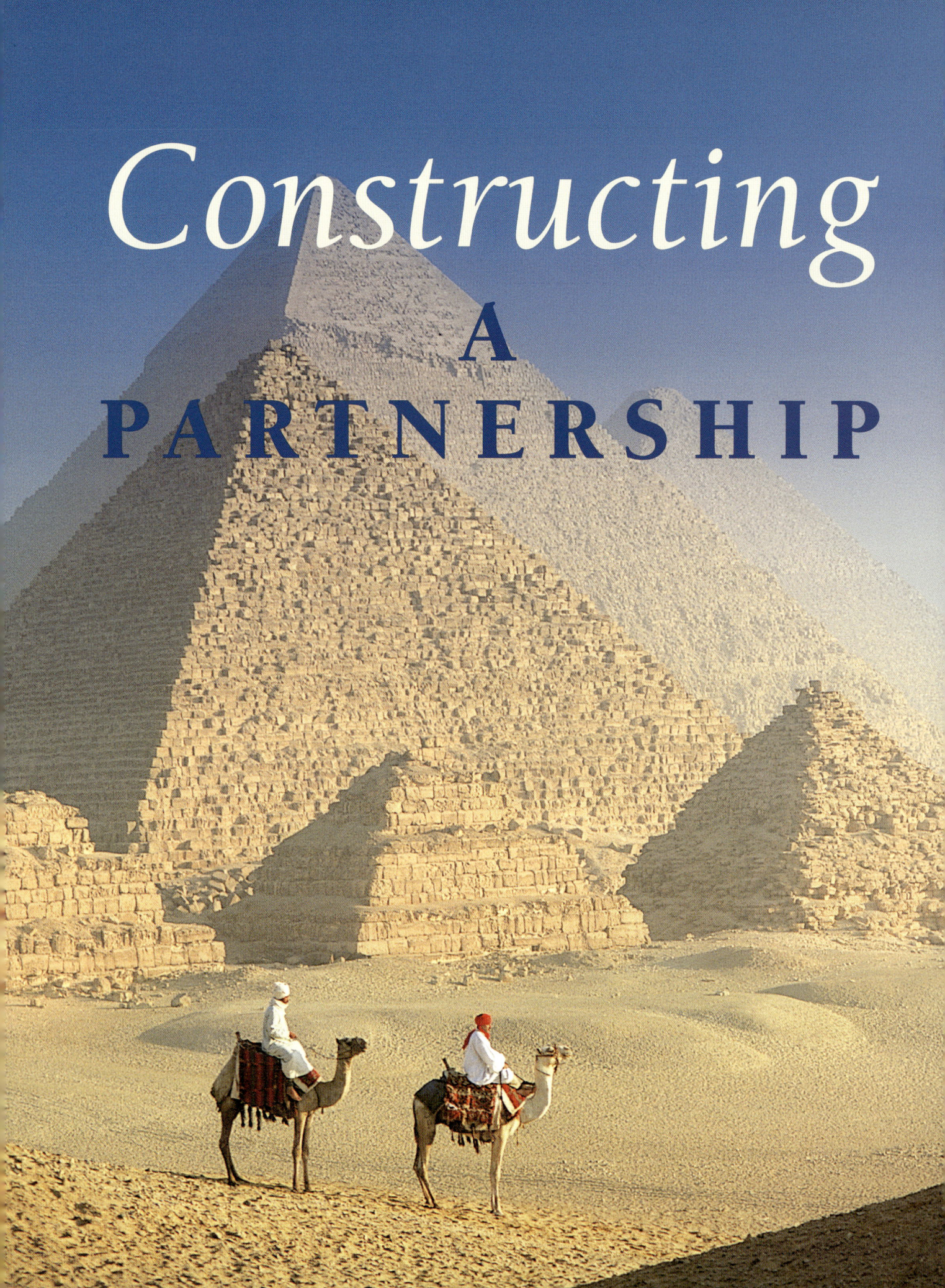

M. CHRISTINE DeVITA
President
The Wallace Foundation
New York, NY

No matter their size or mission, nonprofit organizations need and deserve boards and staff that can openly discuss successes and challenges so that, together, they can help the organization be effective. That is the essence of a constructive partnership. A constructive partnership, in turn, is an essential element of a high-functioning board.

Creating a climate of openness, and the transparency that accompanies it, is critical to nonprofit organizational success, especially in an era marked by heightened accountability for performance and, in many cases, increased competition for resources. That climate depends on a shared agreement of the distinctive roles of the board and the chief executive and, by extension, staff. With a shared agreement, these players can take steps to create the "space" for constructive partnerships — by providing the right information at the right time, by promoting board cohesion and candor, and by creating the right meeting structure. By building on a mutual understanding of their respective roles, chief executives and boards can disprove the belief that "effective governance by the board of a nonprofit is a rare and unnatural act," a phrase used by Barbara Taylor, Richard Chait, and Tom Holland in a *Harvard Business Review* article.

All constructive partnerships require agreement on the complementary roles of board and staff. But the line distinguishing those roles may be drawn at very different places for different types of organizations.

For example, a small startup nonprofit organization with a part-time or single staff member needs board members who straddle both sides of the board–staff line, not only working on governance and strategy but also taking on more operational duties, like accounting, stuffing envelopes for a fundraising mailing, or securing publicity for an event.

At the other end of the continuum, a large nonprofit with many full-time staff would likely draw the line at a different place, with board members focusing more on governance, strategy, and performance assessment, leaving staff members to use their professional expertise to manage the day-to-day operations and implement the approved program initiatives.

Exactly where the line is drawn between board and staff responsibilities will depend on what the organization most needs at its particular stage of development. But wherever it is drawn, the important thing is that the roles and responsibilities of board and staff are clearly discussed and agreed upon. Once this foundation is in place, we've learned that maintaining and enhancing a constructive partnership requires attention to three key areas.

Filling the information gap

The first and perhaps most important component of constructive partnerships is bridging the inevitable information gap that occurs between staff members who live and breathe the organization every day and board members who come together sporadically for a relatively brief time. To effectively fill that gap, nonprofit staff needs to provide information that goes beyond reporting on past events and permits the board to contribute to future decision making in a timely manner. Getting this balance right is a process of constant adjustment. Too much information and board members may feel overwhelmed, even irritated; they may see only trees and miss the forest. Too little information and board members may feel that they can't see the road they're on or whether it is even leading to the forest.

In either case, candor is critical to creating a climate characterized by ongoing commitment to understand and analyze why things went well or poorly so that the organization can keep improving. A candid framing by staff of the situation can provide internal clarity about the relevant issues and make it easier for board members to find an entry point into the decision-making process. At the Wallace Foundation, such candid conversations about the strengths and weaknesses of various strategies have resulted not only in better strategies developed with board input but also greater board engagement and investment in our work as a whole.

And don't underestimate the importance of communicating with board members between meetings. Periodic updates on progress and plans, or requests for advice, keep the board connected to the organization's work between meetings.

Building board cohesion

Because candor is difficult to achieve and sustain without a climate of mutual respect, time invested in helping the board come together as a team pays big dividends. It is important to provide time for board members to get to know one another and to have shared experiences. Like many organizations, Wallace schedules board dinners the night before a board meeting, often inviting an outside speaker whose contributions are relevant to the next day's discussion. We often include senior staff, many of whom regularly present to the board.

Providing opportunities for the board to discuss issues privately is also an important way to build board cohesion and to re-inforce the expectation that all board members are active participants at meetings, not just passive recipients of staff reports. Because staff members generally shape the meeting agenda, it's important for board members to "own" some meeting time that is theirs alone. At Wallace, the board meets in executive session at the beginning and end of every board meeting, once with the chief executive and once without. These sessions provide predictable space and time for board members to ask questions or raise concerns about particular issues that may need attention. The results of these discussions often help shape future meeting agendas. In addition, the board annually discusses its own performance, including whether there has been adequate candor and active participation in board discussions.

Creating the right meeting structure

The third component of constructive partnerships is ensuring board meetings focus on what is most important to the organization's success so that board time is productive and the contributions of board members are maximized. At the Wallace Foundation, our board's most important contribution is guidance on key strategic and performance issues — including the broad program areas in which we invest, the specific goals and strategies to be used in each area, the timing and duration of our initiatives, and our progress in meeting our mission (see sidebar).

THE WALLACE FOUNDATION

Our mission is to enable institutions to expand learning and enrichment opportunities for all people. We do this by supporting and sharing effective ideas and practices. To achieve our mission, we have three objectives:

* Strengthen education leadership to improve student achievement.
* Improve after-school learning opportunities.
* Build appreciation and demand for the arts.

We plan our meeting agendas to allow ample time for strategic and performance issues. At our January meeting, we review the progress of the past year and plans for the coming year. We have developed an annual State of the Foundation Report that functions as an internal scorecard for this purpose. For each of the three other meetings, we do a "deep dive" into one of our three focus areas, reviewing original goals and strategies, results to date, lessons learned, and options for moving forward. The background materials prepared for these discussions are sent at least a week in advance to ensure board members have time to reflect on the issues to be discussed.

At the meeting itself, staff presentations are limited to general framing comments, and most of the time is spent in conversation with the board, answering questions raised, and listening to various perspectives expressed on the issues presented.

It's important to note that we developed this approach in consultation with our board as a result of candid conversation in executive session. We all agreed we needed to provide more time for thinking ahead and reflection — something we observed was difficult when meetings were organized solely around specific recommendations for action. Now, we seek to create "space" for discussions with the board around the strategies that will ultimately drive the recommendations, while still allocating shorter blocks of time for other updates, reviewing financial performance, and voting on specific grants.

Why bother?

Building a constructive partnership between board and staff is not easy (and perhaps not common). From the chief executive's perspective, it takes time to develop the trust that candor requires, and it takes courage to admit to a room full of smart board members that things don't always turn out as planned or that mistakes have been made. From the board's perspective, it takes dedication and commitment to faithfully attend board meetings and to adequately review board materials in advance. And it requires a real investment of time and effort for board members to understand the issues facing an organization so they can help develop the right strategies and performance measures to ensure success.

But the benefits of creating a constructive partnership are well worth the effort. Board members who feel they are active contributors to the organization's success are more engaged and supportive. They are able to more effectively represent the organization to various outside groups, which often results in greater visibility and support for the organization's work. Recruitment becomes easier because new board candidates are attracted to the energy and enthusiasm displayed by current members. From the staff's perspective, the organization's work is strengthened through the counsel of board members. And there is real satisfaction and confidence in knowing that the strategies being implemented have the full understanding and endorsement of the board. And, most importantly, the organization benefits by making full use of the contributions of both board and staff — however the lines are drawn between the two.

In other words, the actions of both board and staff, in partnership, "construct" a more effective organization. And that, in turn, benefits the people across the country whose opportunities for education, enrichment, health, and overall quality of life depend in important part on the vigor and effectiveness of the nonprofit sector.

Reprinted from Board Member®, *Volume 15, Number 5, September/October 2006.*

It's Lonely at the Top

JOSHUA MINTZ
Partner
Cavanaugh, Hagan, Pierson
& Mintz, Inc.
Washington, DC

The selection of the chief executive is among the most important responsibilities of the nonprofit board. Boards take great care — and invest significant time and resources — to establish search committees, identify the skills and experience the ideal candidate should possess, and conduct the interview and selection process.

Once the "perfect" candidate is found and hired, however, these critical conversations about the expectations for the chief executive's performance often stop — and the chief executive is deprived of the feedback needed to be successful in his or her leadership role.

There are many reasons why boards should conduct the periodic assessment of the chief executive. But in our work, three stick out.

It's lonely at the top: The executive's position within the organization, with no peers and no direct supervisor, makes it difficult for him or her to obtain honest feedback to use as a basis for improving performance. "What am I doing well?" and "What can I do better?" are questions that effective leaders want to know — but that often go unanswered. The assessment process provides one of the few opportunities the executive has to obtain insight into his or her strengths, limitations, and overall performance.

If only I'd known: Here's a common refrain I hear from many chief executives: "If I had known they expected that, I would have focused on it!" Boards must clarify their expectations for the chief executive. If the chief executive and the board have not agreed on the executive's priorities for the year, the executive establishes his or her own priorities, which may not be aligned with the board's. Conflict is sure to follow. The assessment process provides the board and chief executive with an opportunity to discuss and agree upon the executive's priorities for the year ahead — as distinct from the organization's priorities — and helps to ensure that everyone shares common expectations for performance.

A chance to say "Well done": The assessment of the chief executive is not intended to be a "gotcha" moment. While some may consider the purpose of assessment to find fault or problems, most boards enter the process with a positive outlook and a desire to strengthen the performance and effectiveness of the chief executive — thereby strengthening the organization as a whole. In many cases, the outcome of the assessment is a strong endorsement of the executive's performance, which serves to re-energize the chief executive and affirm that he or she — and the organization — is headed in the right direction.

By failing to adequately evaluate the chief executive, many nonprofit boards miss an opportunity to ensure that performance expectations between the board and chief executive are clear, to strengthen his or her performance, and to express support for the executive. Neglect can be costly, resulting in mistrust, strained working relationships, ongoing poor performance, and even turnover.

Given its importance, why is the assessment of the chief executive so often neglected? The most common reasons we hear from boards include

- "It requires too great a commitment of time and energy. Let the next board chair deal with the performance issues."

- "Why open a can of worms when things seem to be going along okay?"
- "I don't feel comfortable giving the executive feedback. After all, he (or she) is more of an expert than the board on the organization's issues."
- "Board members have different assessments of the chief executive's performance. The process would likely trigger conflict among the board that I'd prefer to avoid."

In addition to board reluctance, some chief executives don't push for having an assessment because they

- "Don't really want the feedback."
- "Don't think that the board has the information to fairly assess me."
- "Don't want the board to begin micro-managing me."

But most often, boards simply don't know where to begin. While it may sound like a cliché, as the ancient saying goes, "A journey of 1,000 miles begins with a single step." Here are the step-by-steps boards and chief executives should follow on the assessment journey.

1. **Agree to conduct the assessment.** As obvious as this may sound, the assessment process can be a stressful experience for the person being assessed — especially if it comes as a surprise. The assessment process can be initiated by either the board or the chief executive. No matter who starts it, everyone involved needs to be informed. The board and the chief executive should have an opportunity to discuss the assessment. When possible, the chief executive should have input into the design of the process.

2. **Decide how the assessment will be conducted.** One size does not fit all when it comes to assessing the chief executive. Some boards hold interviews with every board member to obtain input. Others use surveys that ask board members to rate performance in specific areas. Open-ended questionnaires provide another vehicle for board member input, though they require more effort on the part of board members in both responding to the survey and summarizing the findings. The best assessment process is the one that fits the needs and culture of your organization.

3. **Agree on what will be asked.** The board (or subgroup of the board) along with the chief executive should develop the assessment questions and ensure that they are relevant and appropriate to the organization. The chief executive's job description and annual performance goals are the place to start. The questions should focus on the chief executive's annual goals, his or her core roles and responsibilities, and the personal leadership skills that the board and executive feel are essential for success in the position. Open-ended questions that focus on the chief executive's greatest successes over the past year and suggested priorities for the year ahead also make great questions. Often, the process of identifying the questions — and determining what the board really thinks is critical — is the most important and enlightening part of the assessment process.

4. **Conduct the assessment and analyze the results.** Distribute the assessment instrument to board members and the chief executive (or complete the interviews). The chief executive should answer the same questions as board members in order to provide a common language for discussion and a basis for comparison between the board's and the executive's perceptions of his or her strengths, limitations, and performance over the past year. The information should be compiled and reported in a way that promotes candor and ensures anonymity.

5. **Review the results with the chief executive and develop an action plan for the upcoming year.** For the assessment process to have real value, it is essential that the board chair, the executive committee, or another assigned board member sit down with the chief executive and discuss the results. What are the major strengths to be built upon? What areas of weakness need to be addressed? What are the critical priorities for the year ahead? While the assessment results provide a starting point for discussion, the primary focus of the conversation should be on the future: What will the chief executive do over the upcoming year to address these issues and improve his or her performance — and how can the board be most supportive in this effort?

The main objective of the assessment process is to encourage self-discovery, professional development, and performance improvement. Personal and professional growth is challenging for all of us. After completing the assessment process and preparing an action plan for the chief executive's development, the board must actively support the chief executive over the next year as he or she works to implement the action plan.

Remember: It really is lonely at the top. While the chief executive is typically surrounded by people — board members, staff members, funders, and stakeholders — he or she is often isolated from information about his or her own performance. The board assessment of the chief executive is one of the most important — and sometimes the only — vehicles for the executive to obtain input into his or her performance. It is a critical process for the executive's and the organization's success, and an essential function of the nonprofit board.

Reprinted from Board Member®, *Volume 13, Number 8, December 2004.*

Frequently Asked Questions about Executive Compensation

BRIAN H. VOGEL
Senior Principal
Quatt Associates, Inc.
Washington, DC

CHARLES W. QUATT
President
Quatt Associates, Inc.
Washington, DC

Q: What are the trends toward making nonprofit salaries competitive?

A: Nonprofit salaries have risen over the last decade, and at least among larger and more complex nonprofits, the gap in salary compensation between for-profits and nonprofits has certainly narrowed. Moreover, some pay practices, such as bonus and deferred compensation, formerly seen only in for-profit organizations, are now increasingly common in nonprofit organizations.

That said, nonprofit total compensation still lags behind for-profit pay, and probably always will. In part this is because nonprofits cannot offer equity or other lucrative forms of long-term compensation. The larger reason, however, is that external scrutiny, federal and state oversight, and the internal culture of nonprofits generally discourage the payment of very high levels of compensation. For many nonprofits, financial considerations are also significant limits on executive pay.

The bottom line: Many nonprofits are now appropriately competitive — paying enough to ensure they can hire the talent they need, but not so much that they risk violating the public trust that expects them to focus on their main responsibility, their mission.

Q: What issues that nonprofits face in compensation are the same as or different from those that for-profits face?

A: Both for-profits and nonprofits face the challenge of balancing the market for executive talent against their internal resources.

Nonprofits increasingly are able to use many of the same tools as for-profits in paying their executives. They can use bonus and incentive pay if they wish, and are able to offer some forms of deferred compensation. As noted above, base salaries have risen in recent years.

Nevertheless, nonprofits continue to operate under stricter constraints than for-profit organizations. As a result, total compensation at nonprofits remains generally below for-profit levels. Nonprofits face stronger public scrutiny and special legal oversight, through the IRS intermediate sanctions rules and other legal limits on compensation. Nonprofits cannot offer some of the most lucrative features of for-profit compensation, such as equity. Deferred compensation is subject to different, and stricter, rules for nonprofits. Bonus plans are less common, and when they exist, generally not as rich. Many nonprofits are also restrained in their pay practices by their mission, their culture, and donor and community expectations.

Q: How do nonprofits determine salaries for chief executives?

A: A step-by-step process for determining chief executive salaries includes

- Reviewing, and if necessary revising, the chief executive title and job description
- Reviewing organizational strategy and objectives and understanding how they connect with chief executive objectives and compensation
- Developing a compensation philosophy to guide decision making
- Understanding and researching the appropriate marketplace
- Understanding and complying with legal requirements
- Understanding and meeting the test of public scrutiny
- Choosing the appropriate level and mix of compensation, including base pay, extra cash compensation (such as bonuses and incentives), deferred compensation, and benefits and perquisites
- Documenting the compensation process and decision

Q: Should the entire board be aware of and/or approve the chief executive's salary and benefits each year?

A: The entire board should be aware of the chief executive's salary and benefits. A board may choose to seek advice from an outside expert when considering in detail and approving the chief executive salary and benefits. Only independent board members, however, should be involved in the final approval process.

Q: Which laws should the board be familiar with when setting the chief executive's salary?

A: Board members need to be familiar with the IRS intermediate sanctions rules and related legal doctrines, such as the private inurement doctrine. They also need to understand the state law applying to their nonprofit. If the board considers deferred compensation arrangements, it needs to understand the federal tax law governing such arrangements.

Q: What is the IRS text on intermediate sanctions?

A: The intermediate sanctions rules are included in Internal Revenue Code Section 4958. The Internal Revenue Service Instructions for Form 990 includes an informative discussion of the intermediate sanctions regulations. (See www.irs.gov/instructions/ for more information.)

Q: We are in the process of evaluating our chief executive. How do we link this to compensation?

A: The best way to link compensation to performance is to decide before the evaluation the rewards associated with achieving your organization's objectives. Thus, you could agree with the chief executive that achieving stated objectives would mean (finances allowing) a certain percentage increase in salary, or the award of an incentive amount. Going beyond the objectives would be worth more.

In the absence of an existing link between pay and performance, the next best thing is to decide on an appropriate reward (a salary increase, an ad hoc bonus, or some combination of the two) and carefully explain to the chief executive the particular achievements that justify the boost in pay. That explanation could then serve as the basis for the following year's performance plan. Remember that any bonus or salary increase must not increase compensation by so much that it creates intermediate sanctions concerns.

Excerpted from Dollars and Sense: The Nonprofit Board's Guide to Determining Chief Executive Compensation *by Brian H. Vogel and Charles W. Quatt, Ph.D. BoardSource, 2005.*

Teamwork That Works

GEORGE C. BENSON
Executive Director
Michigan State University
Foundation
East Lansing, MI

EDWARD JAMES
Board Chair
Michigan State University
Foundation
East Lansing, MI

Having worked together and with numerous other institutions over the years, we have learned that organizations that thrive and get the most done are under the leadership of chief executives and boards with strong, mutually supportive working relationships. The capabilities of each complement the other, enabling the partners to work as a true team. If one has less opportunity to contribute to the work at hand, less will be achieved.

But in what ways does each contribute? Are there clearly defined roles? Do these roles help enhance the partnership? We think so. We believe that an effective board is drawn from and represents the institution's constituency and should, therefore, be its strongest voice. The board is the primary agent of accountability but also adds expertise of great value that cannot reside in any one person alone. In turn, an effective chief executive is the embodiment of the organization's management, with intimate knowledge of its operations, finances, and programs. The chief executive is connected to the environment in which the institution operates and is the first to see danger and opportunity as they loom on the horizon.

Great chief executives and boards function as colleagues, partners, equals — what Peter Drucker called a "double-bridge team." In these roles, they are foils for, play off of, and fortify each other. They depend on one another and judiciously exercise their respective strengths toward common goals. This collaborative equality can only flourish when the two 1) share the same strong, passionate affinity to mission, 2) jointly develop strategy for fulfilling that mission, and 3) work as a team to implement that strategy.

Team building

For our foundation, the buy-in at these three levels originated more than a decade ago when rapidly changing circumstances (driven by an unexpected surge of patent income on two drug therapies developed at the university) forced us to re-examine our mission and strategic direction. The foundation's value to the university was about to increase dramatically because it would soon have the financial capacity to pursue opportunities previously beyond our reach. We needed to decide which to pursue, which to postpone, and where to focus our institutional energies. Doing this right would require close collaboration with our constituency (the university community), which in turn would require the chief executive and board members to figure out how to reach consensus in an environment where there was a powerful sense of commitment but not unanimity.

Of course, this was easier said than done. Early on, there seemed to be as many ideas and convictions about what the foundation was and what it should be as there were members of the board. In several areas, there were clear divergences of opinion that could easily have devolved into impasse or even a tug of war over control. For example, there were fundamental questions about how the foundation's increased financial capacity should be managed: Would it be better to save most of it as an endowment for the future, or were the university's immediate needs so pressing that a substantial sum should be committed to address them? Similarly, we had to decide where to focus the foundation's program of grantmaking. Some felt it would be better to evolve into a research-centered foundation with a large component of support for development of technologies with commercial potential, since these were the primary sources of our income. Others believed that continuing as a broad-based supporter of the university in all its aspects was more appropriate, especially since many outstanding programs had few sources of support outside the foundation.

Fortunately, there was a pragmatic consensus among the majority that the implications for the future were too important to allow differing ideas and opinions to lead to discord. Board members agreed that the best approach was an open re-evaluation, from the ground up, with full participation by the chief executive and the board, allowing every voice to be heard in the process. It began by asking each board member and the executive director to articulate their views of the foundation and its future while everyone just listened. This collegial "clearing of the air" was a powerful tool in ensuring that everyone was included from the outset. It set a tone of openness and transparency for the entire process. We would return to this type of open roundtable when critical issues were discussed because it also enabled the best ideas to rise to the surface and be improved by the dialogue that followed.

Partnering to get the work done

The complexities of our foundation — as fiduciary, grantmaker, real estate developer, and supporter of commercializing technologies developed at the university — meant we

would have to do substantial work to assess our activities and their place in a rearticulated mission. There was so much to do that we had no choice but to recruit each board member into one or more working groups.

The agenda, timeline, and process for re-evaluating our mission and strategic direction became joint responsibilities of the executive committee and chief executive, in collaboration with a talented consultant/facilitator. The chief executive took on the central role of briefing each board working group, gathering extensive information critical to decision making, disseminating it to the board in manageable quantities in a timely way, and serving as ombudsman to the process. In turn, the board's role was to make the best use of this knowledge in evaluating alternatives. The higher the quality of the information, the more the process became one of iteration and dialogue between the chief executive and the board.

The process wasn't always smooth or without interruption. It took nine months of near-total immersion to complete the task of re-examining our mission and strategic direction. It was from the division of labor that a sense of teamwork emerged. Without a doubt, the most valuable byproduct of the process was the new way in which the chief executive and board began to work together. Their transparent process became the basis for the strong partnership that exists today — a partnership based on shared mission, strategy, and teamwork, all driven by a collegial free flow of information and ideas.

Reprinted from Board Member®, *Volume 15, Number 5, September/October 2006.*

SUPPORT YOUR BOARD

Think of it as "enlightened self-interest." Chief executives who take steps to support their boards usually find that their jobs become easier in the process. Of course, the organization is the real beneficiary of a mutually supportive chief executive–board partnership, which is reason enough for chief executives to support their boards by doing the following:

* **Initiate and maintain a structure for board work.** Send out meeting notices, agendas, and other materials well ahead of time. Make sure accurate minutes are taken and distributed later.
* **Show consideration and respect toward board members and facilitate interaction in board relationships.** Take time to understand the positions, concerns, and interests of individual board members and what each finds rewarding or valuable about serving on your board.
* **Provide helpful and useful information to the board.** Your goal should be to make board members feel smart, not to stupefy them with overwhelming amounts of unedited material. Edit, simplify, and clarify information you give to the board.
* **Promote board accomplishments and productivity.** Recognize and acknowledge good performance. Board members are more likely to follow through on commitments if they see examples of other board members who do so.
* **Envision change and innovation with the board.** Keep your board informed of trends and changes in the external environment and their implications for your organization and the work of your board. Use your position to encourage ongoing adaptation and improvement.

Adapted from The Nonprofit Chief Executive's Ten Basic Responsibilities *by Richard L. Moyers. BoardSource, 2006.*

2

MISSION DRIVEN [2]

Exceptional boards shape and uphold the mission, articulate a compelling vision, and ensure the congruence between decisions and core values.

DIMENSION

- **MISSION AND VISION** Exceptional boards put into words the reason why the organization exists and what it hopes to accomplish. With the chief executive, they also develop a compelling vision of where the organization is headed. Board members use a clearly defined mission and vision as a guide and litmus test for all board decisions to ensure the organization is meeting community needs. With staff, they articulate organizational values and translate them into action.

KEITH TIMKO
President
Leader to Leader Institute
New York, NY

Since the Leader to Leader Institute was founded in 1990 as the Peter Drucker Foundation for Nonprofit Management, the social sector landscape has seen significant changes. The numbers of nonprofits have swelled, and management and leadership resources available to social sector leaders have increased dramatically. Despite the emergence of new leadership approaches, one tried and true concept has undergone little change: the centrality of the mission.

The mission remains the foremost organizing tool, helping to build common understanding and ensuring that programs and activities are aligned. For every organization, the mission explains why the organization exists and provides direction for doing the right things.

The mission statement, crafted and wordsmithed to perfection to keep it short and powerful, is the written expression of that mission. Like the coxswain in rowing, the mission statement helps to steer the boat and provides motivation and encouragement to the crew. As Frances Hesselbein, co-founder of our organization, is fond of saying: "Mission is the star we steer by. Everything begins with mission. Everything flows from mission."

The board chair and chief executive — as the leadership team — are the foremost stewards of the mission. (Drucker wrote: "The first job of the leader is to think through and define the mission of the institution.") The most successful leadership teams find organizational approaches that continually revisit and re-affirm the mission of the organization. They find ways of inspiring passion for the mission, communicating the organization's core purpose, and measuring performance relative to the mission. In short, they find a way to live their mission and to make it a part of their organizational DNA.

Passion for the mission

Social sector startups begin with a great deal of passion and zeal for the mission. What they lack in structure and systems, they make up for with a palpable and very personal sense of purpose. However, once organizations have outgrown a core group of founding board members and staff, they need to foster a real connection with and passion for the mission. Organizations that truly live their mission begin first and foremost with passion.

> **DO YOU NEED TO REVISE YOUR MISSION STATEMENT?**
>
> * Is it short (17 or fewer words) and sharply focused? Would it fit on a T-shirt?
>
> * Do board members and staff know the mission statement? Is it clear and easily understood?
>
> * Does it define why you do what you do?
>
> * Does it provide direction for doing the right things?
>
> * Does it inspire your passion and commitment?
>
> * Does it say, in the end, what you want to be remembered for?
>
> * Have you revisited your mission statement in the last three years?

One strategy for maintaining passion for the mission is to make it an explicit component of board and staff recruitment. Instead of focusing narrowly on skill sets and overlooking the passion (or lack thereof) of candidates, one environmental organization deliberately begins all interviews with the mission. Job candidates are encouraged to write about their passion for the mission in applications and cover letters. During an interview, staff members ask candidates about their commitment to the mission. Best-selling business author Jim Collins understands that this mission-based approach to recruitment helps to "get the right people on the bus" and builds enthusiasm and excitement for achieving organizational goals.

Once new board and staff members have joined an organization, orientation is an ideal opportunity to inspire enthusiasm for the mission. For example, the leadership team of a suburban county library reworked its orientation to make it more inspiring for new board members. Previously, orientation had consisted of an introduction to library regulations, but this approach didn't seem to establish the board's central role of stewardship of the institution's mission. Now, during the revamped orientation, new board members are instead engaged in a thought-provoking discussion of the mission. By centering orientation around questions similar to those posed here in "Do You Need To Revise Your Mission Statement?" the board immediately understood its vital role and connected with the mission of the organization: To enrich people's lives with information and cultural resources.

Communicating the mission

Once the mission is in place within an organization, board members, staff, volunteers, funders, vendors, and customers benefit from frequent reminders of the organization's core purpose. For instance, when people walk into your organization, do they see signs of the mission statement? Is it displayed anywhere in your organization's physical offices? Does the mission statement appear on your organization's Web site and in annual reports and newsletters? The following approaches to communicating the mission remind stakeholders of the purpose of their work and their goals.

- Physical plant: In the entrance to ServiceMaster's corporate headquarters, the mission of the organization is showcased in stone. In many public schools, a mission statement prominently displayed in the front entrance greets students, parents, teachers, and administrators and quickly establishes a common point of reference.

- Web site: Project Hope works to achieve sustainable advances in health care around the world, and employees ensure that the words "health opportunities for people everywhere" are visible on every page of their Web site.

- Board and staff meetings: At KaBOOM! — whose mission is to create great playspaces through the participation and leadership of communities — biweekly staff conference calls include reading thank-you letters and stories from children to illustrate how the organization lives its mission.

- Business cards and printed literature: Many organizations print the mission statement on their business cards. It not only reminds employees of why they come to work, it sends a message to those outside the organization that says "this is who we are and what we stand for." Business cards are no longer just for staff. One Make-a-Wish Foundation chapter also prints business cards for board members.

The value of communicating the mission is re-inforced by an often-told story of a NASA custodian who was proud of his work cleaning and polishing floors. When asked to describe his job, he didn't say, "I clean the floors." Instead, he replied, "I help to put men on the moon." Organizations that truly live their mission help everyone — from the chair of the board to volunteers to new program associates — understand at a fundamental level how individual work connects to the mission of the organization.

REVISITING THE MISSION

In 1999, the Girl Scouts Arizona Cactus Pine Council engaged in a strategic planning process using the Drucker Self-Assessment Process. This process asks organizations to consider five questions to focus their energies, listen to their customers, and measure results:

- What is your mission?
- Who is your customer?
- What does the customer value?
- What are your results?
- What is your plan?

Prior to the self-assessment, the Arizona Cactus Pine Council's mission statement was: "To inspire in girls the highest levels of character, conduct, patriotism and service, empowering them to develop a sense of their own self-worth, to achieve their full potential, and to prepare them for the realities of a changing world." As part of the self-assessment, Council members were asked to scrutinize this mission statement to see if it still reflected the organization's beliefs.

Board members, staff, volunteers, and Girl Scouts were asked to identify three words that described what girls got out of participating in Girl Scouts. These words rose to the top of the list: courage, trust, responsibility, leadership, confidence, character, compassion, integrity, and fun. Surveys and additional customer research were done to add to the picture of the organization.

Next, a self-assessment team with clarity about the core values, purpose, and goals of the Girl Scouts Council convened to revisit the mission statement and subsequently proposed this revised version: "To create confidence, conviction, courage, and compassion in girls." The team sent the revised mission statement to the board of directors, which approved it.

How was the team able to accomplish its goal? In the process of revisiting their mission, the Council had reflected on why their organization exists, what their purpose is, and what they wanted to be remembered for. They had focused on creating a short, powerful mission statement that could become "the star they steer by." The focus and clarity of that mission statement has kept the board and staff focused on core priorities and desired results, and, six years later, the National Girl Scouts board of directors has proposed a revised mission statement very similar to the mission adopted by the Girl Scouts Arizona Cactus Pine Council.

Connecting mission and results

Board members, staff, and volunteers who have a passion for the mission also want to know that their efforts are achieving results. Like the coxswain, the leadership team of the board chair and chief executive has a responsibility to inform the crew of where they are in relation to other crews and the finish line. Leaders understand that progress reports on results — and particularly the right results given the mission of the organization — are linked organically to living the mission.

With that in mind, leaders who live the mission strive for new and more comprehensive ways to measure their results. They yearn for new sources of information and continually seek input from the board, staff, volunteers, and customers about how they can be more effective in delivering their programs and services. Frequently, these organizations have feedback loops, established indicators, customer surveys, and periodic evaluations that apprise the leadership team of how well the organization is furthering its mission.

Organizations that live their mission also expend considerable effort on increasing staff understanding of the connection among personal accountability, mission, and results of the organization. For instance, the environmental organization cited earlier includes "furthering the mission" as the first accountability item in all board and staff position descriptions. Annual performance reviews are an opportunity to revisit the staff's passion for the mission and to emphasize the connection between daily tasks and the organization's results. Volunteers and staff can then say with confidence, "This is how I contribute to the goals of the organization."

Reading Is Fundamental, a literacy organization, connects an individual's efforts with the overall mission of the organization by encouraging employees to use company time to volunteer with literacy organizations. As volunteers, staff members are able to further the organization's mission of preparing and motivating children to read while being reminded of the vital connection between their work and the organization's goals of promoting literacy.

For organizations to effectively live their mission, they need a board and staff who are passionate about the mission, whether it is eradicating poverty, promoting social justice, or protecting the environment. Once those stakeholders are equipped with a solid understanding of the organization's mission and know that results are being achieved, the entire board and staff are engaged as champions for the organization. Whether the work is raising money or putting together board books, their passion is tapped, their enthusiasm for the work irrepressible, and, suddenly, by living the mission, the organization's bright path into the future is in focus.

Reprinted from Board Member®, *Volume 14, Number 4, August/September 2005.*

Vermont Foodbank Stays True to Its Mission

DEBORAH A. FLATEMAN
Chief Executive Officer
Vermont Foodbank
Barre, VT

The Vermont Foodbank has always been a mission-driven organization, more so than any other nonprofit I've been involved with either as a volunteer or paid staff member. This has always been apparent on the board level, too. The people we attract to serve are not motivated by social appearances or the clout of serving with others who are high profile. The people we attract are high profile, but most importantly, have a genuine passion for our work. (We once had a board member who was so distraught by the idea that children were going hungry that she wanted to make peanut butter and jelly sandwiches to pass out to kids on the street!) This passion has been a tradition, and I'm happy to say that it still is.

Reconnecting to mission

When I came to the Foodbank eight years ago, I found an exciting opportunity. It appeared that the Foodbank was ready for radical growth. Everywhere I looked there were untapped resources and underdeveloped initiatives. We set about the business of growing our operation, perfecting systems, and in general, rising to a higher level of function. Our board, however, seemed to be in limbo; the founding board (what I would characterize as volunteers serving as staff — very hands-on) was long gone. Board members had gone through a successful executive search and were thinking about what they would focus on next.

They knew that "hands-on" was inappropriate; passion for our mission compelled all of us to find ways to re-engage the board in our work. We decided to re-establish a committee structure with the requirement that each member serve actively in some way. This worked for a while until we weathered a major catastrophe — our roof collapsed under ice and rain, making one-third of our warehouse unusable. This single event brought us together in a new way. In 23 months we successfully raised funds for and built a new facility. No time for feasibility studies or major donor cultivation!

I had heard that boards often function best in a crisis, and I saw this firsthand. If any good can come out of a roof collapsing, it might be that this catastrophe reconnected board members and others in a demonstrable way to our mission of distributing food. This tangible connection made it easy for everyone to get involved quickly and to see immediately how their efforts made a big difference to our organization and community.

The Foodbank moved into its new facility in February 2001. By this time our staff had tripled in size, our distribution had quadrupled, and our trucking fleet had grown from two to six. In what seemed like overnight, we were a different organization with plans to continue growing. Today, we still have about 30 staff and are distributing six times what we were eight years ago. Our visibility is higher, our reputation as the antihunger leader in Vermont continues to galvanize us, and within the past two years we've recognized a need to become more sophisticated in how we operate. More and more we find ourselves diligently examining our effectiveness at meeting our mission.

2

Transitioning to policy governance

From the board perspective, Vermont Foodbank is a vibrant organization taking hold under strong leadership and excellent staff. From my perspective, the excitement of the Foodbank's accomplishments needs to be complemented by board activities that support the organization's growth initiatives. What we've all realized is that our board is at its absolute best at our annual retreats, taking on the bigger issues around our mission, our direction, our vision, and our values. This realization has led us to explore the feasibility of employing the Carver model of policy governance.

As our organization has grown, we have improved many of our processes and have added increasingly capable staff. With smoother operations come the ability and desire of the board to focus its attentions on mission in a larger context. To help achieve this, we have spent the last 18 months going through the process of transitioning to policy governance. It has been a lot of hard, rewarding work. Our talented, inspirational board members are now working on a level that befits our organization and their keen abilities. We are about to put into ink our next five-year plan and, simultaneously, to examine, and rewrite if necessary, our mission statement.

Altering the mission statement

Our mission statement was written in 1986, the year of incorporation, and really hasn't been touched since: The mission of the Vermont Foodbank is to end hunger in Vermont by ensuring that everyone has access to enough quality food essential to their nutritional health. It's still accurate, but it reads more like a statement of purpose, i.e., "this is what we do and why we do it," rather than "this is why we are organized to change the world." The current statement doesn't really reflect our personality, our values, or our depth. We are about much more than merely making food accessible. Indeed, our core work and its resulting impact effects societal change that we can barely fathom. So, it makes perfect sense that having gone through the Carver process of establishing who our "owners" are (to whom are we accountable?) and what our "ends" are (desired outcomes), we would also scrutinize our mission statement and possibly alter it to fit our expanding organizational goals.

Despite the fact that our overarching outcome is to end hunger in Vermont, we know that we will not do it alone. How does our mission statement speak to our community, our partnerships, or our role as a cog in the giant wheel of national hunger relief efforts? How does it speak to our taking action to develop and support initiatives around sustainable systems that improve the quality and availability of food in our local region? As an organization, our basic function has not changed, but our wisdom has. Our mission statement must reflect what we have learned in the past 20 years, and what we hope to be in the next 20. It must ring with the inflection of our older-but-wiser voice. It is time to put pen to paper. Luckily our board's inherent flexibility and true commitment to doing what is best for the organization will not only allow this to happen, but the process will be stewarded with care, intelligence, and (oh, what was that word?) passion!

Reprinted from Board Member®, *Volume 14, Number 4, August/September 2005.*

Since this article appeared in Board Member, *Deborah Flateman has become CEO of the Maryland Foodbank. The Vermont Foodbank has adopted the following mission statement: "The mission of the Vermont Foodbank is to gather and share quality food and nurture partnerships that will end hunger in Vermont."*

Vision and Values

KAY SPRINKEL GRACE
Principal
Transforming Philanthropy, LLC
San Francisco, CA

A vision statement is not the same as a mission statement. A mission statement answers the question "Why?" A vision statement is the expression of what you see in the future if your organization is successful at addressing its mission. You need both a vision and a mission. The vision is the inspiration for the organization's plan: It is the destination, and the plan is the road map. The mission is the compass. It is the true north for the organization, the point on which there is full agreement. It serves as the tiebreaker when needed and guides an organization along the right path.

Vision defined

Vision is defined variously. Your vision is your dream. Jim Kouzes and Barry Posner, authors of *The Leadership Challenge,* simply defined a vision as what you want your organization to look like, feel like, be like in the future. Vision is spun from the loftiest goal that you have (and inspires the more attainable goals that frame an institutional plan). Vision is the enticing idea of what could happen to the community you serve (from local to global), to the issue you address ("We envision a time when our research will have eradicated both the causes and ravages of liver cancer."), and to the organization itself if all your ideas were implemented and all your dreams came true. The vision inspires action: planning, fundraising, marketing, good governance, sound management. People want their dreams to come true.

Vision may have two prongs: your vision for your organization ("to be the most respected provider of senior services in our city") and your vision for what your work will accomplish ("We envision a time when no child will be without health insurance, and no neighborhood without health services.")

Values in vision and mission

Values, which are the basis of philanthropy, are embedded in both mission and vision. In the Vector Health Program's mission statement, the values are implicit (work, love, play, comfort), as they need to be in all mission statements. Yale University School of Medicine's statement is also values rich (health, innovation, leadership). Values are what click with people when they read your materials. The vision statements above also have implicit and expressed values.

As boards work to gain a sense of mission and create and re-affirm mission statements, it is imperative to know and communicate values, focus on ways to incorporate values into the mission statement, and keep the three soft drivers of nonprofit success (mission, vision, values) on the board table as much as the hard drivers (money, people, marketing). Indeed, without the soft drivers, the hard ones don't work.

Excerpted from The Nonprofit Board's Role in Setting and Advancing the Mission *by Kay Sprinkel Grace. BoardSource, 2003.*

3

STRATEGIC THINKING [3]

Exceptional boards allocate time to what matters most and continuously engage in strategic thinking to hone the organization's direction.

DIMENSIONS

- **PLANNING** Exceptional boards partner with staff to frame and assess the strategic plan. Drawing on an understanding of organizational strengths and weaknesses, industry trends, and peer benchmarking, they articulate priorities and monitor progress against financial and programmatic goals. After translating strategic priorities into action plans, they use these plans to assess the chief executive, drive meeting agendas, and shape board recruitment.

- **THINKING** Rather than confining strategic thinking to an annual planning process, exceptional boards make it part of regular, ongoing board work. They ask far-ranging questions to help clarify thorny problems, offer break-through insights on pressing issues, present new ways of framing challenges and opportunities, and actively generate important strategic ideas.

THINKING OUTSIDE
THE BOARDROOM

TERRY WILLIAMS
Retired Senior Director
McKinsey & Company
Washington, DC

Imagine two nonprofit boards, A and B. Board A has it all figured out. Agendas are distributed well before meetings, and meetings are efficient and predictable. Financial oversight is handled carefully. Things run smoothly. Occasionally, though, a bad strategic surprise occurs. When it does, the board pulls together with good spirit and does what it can to recover.

Board B operates differently. Meetings are more contentious, a bit livelier. Although it occasionally delves into management issues (when they involve a major financial expense or top personnel matter), mostly the board members are interested in big questions about performance, future funding, how the organization is perceived, how it can improve its service to the community — topics that rarely lead to immediate decisions but definitely establish a strategic agenda for ongoing attention.

Board B engages in strategic thinking most of the time; Board A does not. Board B's discussions go beyond the ordinary process questions to more "thoughtful" inquiries that drive deeper into competitive conditions, constituencies' interests, and value-laden concerns. Board B devotes time to what matters most for the organization and its development. Board A may be "buttoned up" but is much more dependent on its staff for strategic early warnings and proposed actions to be taken.

Can, and should, all boards become more like Board B? I think so. Making strategic thinking a habit takes time, effort, and discipline, but it enables the board to be much more helpful.

What is strategic thinking?

Strategic thinking, in a nutshell, is critical reasoning applied to matters that most influence the future performance and viability of the organization — reasoning at a level of quality and value far above a perfunctory discussion of current conditions. Strategic thinking focuses on what matters most.

Board members individually and collectively can do this if they are both:

- Intentional about improving strategies and performance. Board members explicitly search for issues, topics, and opportunities that will improve and defend the organization strategically. They choose carefully what they spend time on.

- Disciplined about what and how to be thinking. They adopt more effective ways of examining complex and provocative issues. They look at subjects in new ways and from different angles — not just looking backward to see where the organization has come from, or forward when they engage in strategic planning, but over, under, and around the issues. They ask why, what if, and what do others do? They react to and interpret information in ways that lead to clear choices, decisions, and actions.

All of this makes regular "meetings" feel much more like retreats, where members are encouraged to take the time to focus on the big issues. Thoughtful conversations — about the external environment, community needs and perceptions, peers, and competitors — will identify crucial issues and lead to more relevant, timely, and constructive decisions. All this while getting their fundamental fiduciary work done, too.

Strategic thinking vs. strategic planning

Strategic planning is, of course, a vital process and sequence by which strategies are developed. But while planners can describe the plan's table of contents and the required elements of a plan, doing so does not automatically lead to good content, to a competitively superior plan.

Good strategic thinking, on the other hand, does supply the valuable content. It's vital because it contributes to the success of the organization — period! Quality content comes not from participating in environmental scans or SWOT (Strengths, Weaknesses, Opportunities, Threats) analysis but rather from the active brain power of board members and staff applied to pertinent subject matter and analyses. In an article titled "Living Strategy," the authors provide a helpful definition: "Strategic thinking is about inquiry, dialogue, and stories; says you can't predict the future, but you can be ready for whatever it brings by being adaptive; is an ongoing, iterative process; involves collective knowledge and intelligence-gathering capabilities; is organic, systems-oriented thinking; emphasizes conversation as a core process; and becomes a natural part of everyone's present and future work."

Getting started

Done well, strategic thinking makes the board a significantly richer strategic asset. Board work is far more productive and satisfying to board members. And the staff will find it has more time to deal with significant issues, no longer being drawn by the board into operational or inconsequential matters.

The board is uniquely positioned to bring such perspective because of its experience, diversity of background, sectorwide connections, loyalty to the organization and its mission, and detachment from day-to-day operations.

Making strategic thinking an integral part of board behavior takes attention and time. The following suggestions will help you get started:

- Retool your meeting agendas by allocating sufficient time for thinking. Strategic matters take time; rich debate won't flourish if the entire meeting is absorbed in discussing operational issues or those of little strategic consequence. Try using a consent agenda (it groups routine items, such as previous meeting minutes and committee reports, under one umbrella that the board can vote on without additional discussion) so there is time for discussions of important issues. Ask if the right — i.e., most important — items are on the agenda.

- Pose "catalytic questions" or use some other meeting "devices" to stimulate thinking and promote lively, robust debates (see sidebars).

CATALYTIC QUESTIONS

In the book *Governance as Leadership*, the authors suggest posing catalytic questions that invite creativity, exploration, and do not depend largely on data and logic to answer.

* What three adjectives or short phrases best characterize this organization?
* What will be most strikingly different about this organization in five years?
* What do you hope will be most strikingly different about this organization in five years?
* On what list, which you could create, would you like this organization to rank at the top?
* Five years from today, what will this organization's key constituents consider the most important legacy of the current board?
* What will be most different about the board or how we govern in five years?
* How would we respond if a donor offered a $50 million endowment to the one organization in our field that had the best idea for becoming a more valuable public asset?
* How would we look as a take-over target by a potential or actual competitor?
* If we could successfully take over another organization, which one would we choose and why?
* What has a competitor done successfully that we would not choose to do as a matter of principle?
* What have we done that a competitor might not do as a matter of principle?
* What headline would we most/least like to see about this organization?
* What is the biggest gap between what the organization claims it is and what it actually is?

Excerpted from Governance as Leadership by Richard P. Chait, William P. Ryan, and Barbara Taylor. BoardSource and John Wiley & Sons, 2005.

- Challenge others' thoughts and behavior. A useful strategic thought must lead somewhere; it should consciously aim to improve strategic results. Some boards rotate responsibility for a member to play devil's advocate at each meeting to prevent complacency in discussions by challenging assumptions and probing traditional thinking. With practice, this process will become more natural and ingrained as board members see the value such thinking produces.

- Strengthen the board's composition. Does it include people who can look at things differently? If board members are mostly technical, consider recruiting an artist or writer to bring a fresh perspective. Board members who have become jaded or bored may find it difficult to be energetic and creative. Consider new blood.

These suggestions may not magically transform the board into one that thinks strategically. But these ideas can initiate the transition to a high-performing team of board members. Nourished and practiced over time, with the right leadership, they will encourage strategic thinking to naturally occur — almost without thinking.

Reprinted from Board Member®, *Volume 15, Number 2, March/April 2006.*

ROBUST DISCUSSIONS

Try these techniques to stimulate board deliberations that are highly participative and relatively spontaneous.

* **Silent Starts.** Take two minutes at the beginning of the board meeting for members to write (anonymously) the most important questions the board and management should address. Read and tally to identify the most crucial issues.

* **One-Minute Memos.** At the conclusion of each discussion item, board members take a minute to write down what they would have said if there had been more time. Collect for review by the chair and chief executive so there's no doubt about what's on the board's mind.

* **Future-Perfect History.** In breakout groups, develop a future-perfect narrative of how the organization can move from its present state to its envisioned state. Compare story lines and pathways and detours.

* **Counterpoints.** Randomly designate two board members to make the most powerful counterarguments to initial staff recommendations.

* **Role Plays.** Ask subsets of the board to assume the perspective of different constituent groups likely to be affected by the issue at hand. How would they frame the issue and define a successful outcome? What would each group regard as a worst-case scenario?

* **Surveys.** Prior to discussing a major issue, board members take an anonymous survey that includes questions like: What should top our agenda next year? What are we overlooking? What is the most valuable step we could take to be a better board? What are the most/least attractive and worrisome aspects of the proposed strategic plan? An analysis of the responses (not the loudest voice) drives subsequent discussion.

Excerpted from Governance as Leadership *by Richard P. Chait, William P. Ryan, and Barbara Taylor. BoardSource and John Wiley & Sons, 2005.*

Design for the Future: Creating a Strategic Plan That Works

Venture into the office of almost any nonprofit organization, nose around a little bit, and you're bound to find one. Whether it's a carefully organized binder sitting on a chief executive's desk for quick daily reference or a dusty folder crammed with scribbled notes and outlines, it seems like almost everyone has a strategic plan.

The contrast between that organized, well-used binder and the forgotten folder raises a few interesting questions: How do you formulate and implement a practical strategic plan? And, almost equally important, how does a board ensure staff buy-in?

Obviously, most boards embarking on a strategic planning process hope it will become a dynamic guide for the organization. But the line between a plan that is put into action and an aged pile of ideas on a back shelf is thin.

Even if a good plan is drawn up — one that may be used every day to guide decisions — staff buy-in and accountability can be elusive.

Obviously, strategic planning isn't a simple process, and drawing up that first plan is not an easy goal. But those who have been there and those who specialize in such plans say coming up with a useful blueprint that is supported by both staff and volunteers isn't an impossible dream. In fact, they say, it's critical to the success of a nonprofit organization.

Many roads, one destination

Asking for a definition of strategic planning seems like a no-brainer. But different people have very different ideas about what should be included in a strategic plan.

By definition, the process of planning strategically calls for establishing a goal, predicting what forces will help or hinder movement toward that goal, and formulating a plan for achieving it.

Irv Katz, president/CEO of The National Assembly of Health and Human Service Organizations in Washington, D.C., says that defining exactly what a board wants from a plan is an invaluable first step toward creating one. "I view strategic planning as the discipline of determining what role an organization should play in the marketplace in which it operates," Katz says. He cautions that too many organizations fall into the trap of using strategic planning to convince others of the good job they do in the marketplace, rather than trying to clarify and improve upon that job.

"Determining where an organization fits in its environment and how it can maximize its position is the strategic challenge, not convincing people it's a good organization," he says. "Strategic planning is ineffective if the result is a static plan. Continuous strategic thinking and action are essential to keep an organization dynamic in its ever-changing environment."

Strategic planning has been around almost as long as nonprofits, but recent years have brought changes in the way they're written and used.

Doug Eadie, an author and consultant based in Florida, says that the notion of a highly detailed five-year strategic plan is unrealistic in a world that's constantly changing. "Forget doing that kind of five-year plan," he says. "It's really a waste of time. Beyond the first year or so, you get into a kind of la-la land because you don't know what the world is going to do. How can you respond to the world several years out when you don't know how it's going to change?"

Although some organizations still find that a five-year plan is efficient, they are careful to thoroughly review the plan every year or two. Lucy Theilheimer, director of strategic planning for AARP, says their three-to-five-year plan is reviewed almost annually.

"Some elements of it are really long range and deal with our social mission and the impact side of what we do," she says. "We try to bring it closer in by focusing on critical priorities. Overall, our plan bridges three to five years, but we also know that major behavioral changes can take 20 years or more."

Theilheimer says constantly reviewing the plan ensures it remains both dynamic and relevant, taking into consideration changes in the world and the association's marketplace.

"Our strategic planning process requires that we do some level of review and adjustment almost every year," she says. "This year's a big one, and we've opened up the whole plan and reviewed all our new member data. Next year, we'll be more focused on areas that need particular attention. On off years, we review the plan to see if there's anything major we need to look at. We focus on priorities rather than the whole direction of the plan."

Others say that the key to any successful strategic plan is to build in flexibility, which is why some prefer to call it a strategic framework instead of a plan.

"I think one of the keys is flexibility on time," says Stephen Richard, executive director of Arena Stage, a nonprofit theater company based in Washington, D.C. Richard has led his and other arts organizations through strategic planning sessions as a consultant. "An organization similar to ours is looking at a major facility issue that, by its nature, is likely to stretch out beyond their three-year plan. The plan has to take those activities into

consideration. While the operational part of a plan might use a three-year time window, I think there are projects that will extend beyond those three years, and those need to be accommodated."

Building a framework for the future

The most popular way to devise a strategic plan is with an off-site retreat where board members and key staff can gather with an outside consultant or facilitator for an all-day or several-day huddle. But the real work for a retreat begins months before the board and staff meet. That's when consultants are hired and data collected to ensure that any plan meets the needs of the organization.

Most consultants agree that, ideally, the entire strategic planning process should take three to nine months. By the same token, however, they caution against devoting too much time to planning.

Once data have been gathered and background found and condensed into useful reports, organizations are ready to culminate their planning process in a retreat. These take on many forms, from meetings of a few people over breakfast to three- or four-day events with hundreds of participants.

Richard says that holding a retreat not only off-site but some distance away can be a tremendous help. "If you leave the immediate geographic center of an organization and go an hour away, people are less likely to come late and leave early," he notes. "There's a chemistry that happens when people make a commitment to spend a day or a weekend looking hard at a set of issues in their organization."

Even having a day to meet about strategic policies down the street from the office can be enormously helpful. Rosalee Chiara, board chair of Habitat for Humanity of Montgomery County, Maryland, says setting aside a Saturday every other year for two dozen staffers to meet has been essential to her group's strategic planning progress.

Habitat for Humanity of Montgomery County devised its first strategic plan in the mid-1990s. Then, for several years, the all-volunteer organization held a planning meeting every other year to revise and rewrite the plan, keeping it current and dynamic. When the organization hired its first paid staff member last year, however, its board began considering meeting once a year instead.

"It's hard to get all the board members to concentrate," Chiara admits. "It's very hard for people to sit down and focus on all of this. It's not that they don't want to, but it's not a fun thing to do. On the other hand, it's very useful. Everybody feels that the organization has really benefited from it."

At the other end of the spectrum is AARP, which, at press time, was preparing for a four-day meeting that would bring together 450 people to consider the group's plan for the future.

"We'll have a draft strategic plan that will have received input from the executive leadership and the leadership team. The board will have seen it and given comments," says AARP's Theilheimer. "We'll distribute it to the conference participants beforehand. The conference will focus on several things: the present plan overall and what we like and don't like, comments, suggestions, and issues."

At the same time, there will be half-day sessions on three priority areas that are being considered. "It's not a decision-making conference," she says. "It's about informing and generating discussion. As long as you're not trying to get 450 people to agree, you can do it."

Ensuring buy-in

Among the biggest challenges of a strategic plan is ensuring the board and staff are on the same page. It's a common problem, but one that has a simple solution: Make sure staff members are included in the planning process, and they'll likely be motivated to see the plan through.

Mike Allison, director of consulting and research at CompassPoint Nonprofit Services in San Francisco, says it's important to have everyone involved and to be clear about exactly what the staff's role will be. "There's a trap wherein the board pretends or acts like the process is participatory, but really the board is holding the key to final decisions," he says. "The staff may be giving input, but they're not sharing in the final decisions. If that's the case and you're clear about it, most staff can accept it. Where it's a problem is if staff members think they're participating in the decision, but they're really just giving input. There can be a deep sense of disenfranchisement there."

He also recommends having staff set part of the agenda and inviting them to suggest areas that they feel need attention. "Ask them what they think are the most important issues," he says. "If you ask staff to come in and sit at meetings but you don't respond to things they feel are urgent or important, you're likely to erode buy-in. If people are clear about the way they're participating and engaging in issues, they're likely to accept and support the outcomes of the planning process."

Most consultants agree that, in many organizations, it's impossible to include all staff at every planning meeting or during the final retreat. But there are ways to make staff members feel that their voices have been heard. In large organizations where having everyone attend meetings is unrealistic, the staff can be surveyed at individual department meetings.

Department heads then report back to the board or to the planning committee and convey staff ideas and concerns. It may be helpful to have an outside consultant meet with staff members rather than their supervisors. "Sometimes an outside facilitator can be very useful," says Arena Stage's Richard. "It's a little hard for staff members to make suggestions that might be perceived as critical when their bosses are in the room. But those suggestions can be the operational details that make a strategic initiative happen."

Reprinted from Board Member®, *Volume 11, Number 5, May 2002.*

This article was written by former Board Member® *editor John DiConsiglio. He is now a freelance writer. Mike Allison is now an independent consultant. Rosalee Chiara has completed her term as the board chair of Habitat for Humanity of Montgomery County, Maryland.*

Driving Strategic Planning

DEBORAH L. KOCSIS
Consultant
Cornerstone Consulting
Associates, LLC
Granville, OH

SUSAN A. WAECHTER
Consultant
Cornerstone Consulting
Associates, LLC
Granville, OH

The strategic planning process is a management tool designed to improve the effectiveness of an organization. Success is achieved by providing a framework that enables the organization to focus its energy, to coordinate the efforts of its members so that they are working toward the same goals, and to assess the organization's response to changing factors and to adjust accordingly. Strategic planning is, in essence, a disciplined approach to decide what an organization is, what it does, and why it does it, with a focus on the future.

A well-formulated strategic plan must include

- Mission: A statement declaring the purpose of your organization; this statement must be narrow enough to explain succinctly why the organization exists, and broad enough to allow flexibility

- Vision: A statement describing a desirable future state that does not yet exist; the vision provides the different constituencies with a shared sense of where the organization is headed

- Guiding Principles: A list of core values and beliefs about how work is to be accomplished in your organization; these statements express the code of conduct of how people within the organization interact with their colleagues and clients

- Strategies: High-level options for direction to help your organization meet its goals and fulfill its mission

- Goals: The accomplishments that allow your organization to meet its mission-related prerequisites

- Objectives: The purposes and rationale that help your organization further define and support your strategic goals; these are the more immediate aims that need to be realized en route to achieving longer-term goals — interim steps and accomplishments that provide a specific road map

- Tactics: Detailed action steps that support your objectives

- Actions: The tactical items in the day-to-day work of the organization that, if accomplished, will allow your organization to be successful in its plan; detailed actions are defined in separate operational plans

Ten-step strategic planning process

The development of a strategic plan unfolds in a series of discrete stages, each subsequent step building upon the previous ones. The basic 10-step process is

Planning To Plan
1. Assess readiness for planning, define the participants' roles, and decide how to manage the process

Understanding Context
2. Assess the external context: clients, economic factors, social sector issues, and trends

3. Assess the internal context: forces shaping the organization from within

Purpose and Direction
4. Agree on mission (purpose)

5. Agree on vision (direction)

6. Agree on guiding principles (values)

How We Will Get There

7. Generate strategies that fulfill mission, move toward vision, and address the context
8. Create and prioritize goals to support strategies
9. Develop tactics and actions to implement the goals

Monitor the Plan

10. Evaluate progress and update the plan on a regular basis

The players and their roles in strategic planning

Stakeholders

Strategic planning is, or must be, a team effort. Without the input and feedback of all stakeholders — individuals who either depend on or benefit from the services provided by the organization, or who ensure support by financing, overseeing, or implementing the activities — it is difficult to cover all aspects of the organization's future options. While orchestrating the process, the chief executive needs to determine who the relevant stakeholders are at this particular phase in the life of the organization. He or she also needs to pay special attention to defining the role of each participant, at which phase of the process each person is a contributor, and ensuring that a clear communication link exists between the different parties to keep everyone synchronized and informed of the progress.

The chief executive

Among the principal roles in the job description of the nonprofit chief executive is to establish the organization's goals and the proper methods of achieving those goals. Within this context, the chief executive drives the planning process. He or she typically takes the lead in recognizing the need for strategic planning and determining whether the moment is opportune to initiate the planning process.

The role of the chief executive in the strategic planning process is to

- enlist advance support from board members
- prepare board and staff for planning
- coordinate and integrate players' input
- manage the process

In partnership with the chair, the chief executive ensures that the following steps are taken:

- Determine whether to include an outside consultant in the process.
- Designate the responsibilities of the strategic planning task force.
- Establish clear guidelines for membership in the strategic planning task force.

The board

The board is essentially liable for the strategic thinking that is involved in the planning process. The participation of the board in developing the strategic plan is vital since the board is ultimately responsible for setting the direction and mission of the organization, overseeing finances, and contributing to fundraising. Through the board's involvement, the process benefits from extensive conversations among the various stakeholders describing their vision of the organization. As the link between the nonprofit and the outside environment in which the organization functions, the board is in an advantageous position to help reconcile the ambitions of the executive leadership and staff with the restraints of economic and political realities. Because of this great need of guidance and involvement from the board, and the reality that board members tend to come with different perspectives depending on varied levels of involvement in past organizations of different shapes and sizes, consensus on strategy is even more sensitive and imperative.

The benefits to the organization of having the board involved extend past the development of the plan. With the board grounded in the rationale and choices underlying the organization's long-term strategy, it is better able to govern. The strategic plan will eventually guide the board in future decision making; it will facilitate and inspire the board's fundraising efforts; it will help the board better understand how the organization operates.

The following list outlines the demands of the board in the strategic planning process.

- Work together with the chief executive to provide guidance and input in developing the strategic planning process.
- Represent the organization's diverse constituencies within the strategic planning task force, with special emphasis on the community that the nonprofit is mandated to serve. Board members can adapt the process to new information about the community as it may affect the organization.
- Add value to the deliberative discussions by offering professional points of view, which can include legal, financial, marketing, technological, industry-related, and business expertise.
- Contribute to environmental scanning and information gathering by offering information about such things as governance practices, program offerings, organizational initiatives, and technical developments they are familiar with through experience on other boards.
- Offer counsel on the impact that contemplated, strategic initiatives will have on the nonprofit's fiscal viability and fundraising capacity.
- Approve the plan.
- Periodically monitor the success of particular programs and services mandated by the strategic plan.

The staff

The staff is essentially liable for the details of operational planning, constituting the link between the top-level vision of the organization and its everyday activities. Staff is in close proximity to programs and interacts directly with clients and constituents. The presence of key staff representatives on the strategic planning task force is important for several reasons. Mixing the board and staff during planning sessions enables each to share the organizational perspective of the other and better understand their respective concerns. This builds mutual trust. In formulating a course of action for the long term, it is important to consider the frontline experience and professional knowledge of those whose activities will determine success. By providing input during the planning process, staff is able to gain ownership of the ultimate plan that it will be implementing at a later date.

Clients/customers

In discussing the roles or definitions of clients versus customers, these terms tend to be used interchangeably. In most organizations, a customer takes part in the purchase of products, publications, and materials; in the context of this book, clients are more often considered to be the individuals purchasing and participating in the interactive services of the organization, such as patient care and training sessions. The term constituent may refer to any beneficiary or user of services, also commonly substituted for either term discussed above. It is always possible, however, for a funder, the government, or an umbrella organization to become a major client for a nonprofit, purchasing services or products for its own constituents, and thus breaking the connection between the ultimate beneficiary and the nonprofit.

Funders and contributors
Funders and contributors can offer unique contributions to the planning process. If the chief executive is sufficiently confident in his or her relationship with funders, it may be useful to invite several to participate in the planning process (it is important that their counsel be sought judiciously, however, lest their presence distorts the proceedings). As economic conditions become more difficult for nonprofits, it is sensible to consciously consider in strategic conversations whether the objectives of the organization's major and potential funders can be integrated more deeply into the long-term strategy of the nonprofit without compromising its independence. Funding is the means that enables the organization to pursue its mission and not the end in itself.

Facilitator: Do you need a consultant?
Although it is certainly possible to develop an effective strategic plan with a member of the organization responsible for managing the details of the process, the alternative of employing an outside facilitator is always available and sometimes advisable. This is particularly true if the organization has never previously conducted strategic planning.

The primary reason for considering outside facilitation is objectivity. Even the best-intended stakeholder in an organization is likely to have a vested interest in the outcome of some of the issues being discussed and decided. A consultant, on the other hand, can be expected to exercise neutrality since his or her interest is in completing the process itself rather than in the specific content of the plan. A consultant may also be desirable because of his or her past experience in producing strategic plans and credible knowledge in avoiding predictable pitfalls. A consultant acts as a facilitator when directing the process. This facilitator can also offer a general orientation and training to the members of the strategic planning task force to maximize the efficiency of the proceedings and maximize the value of individual contributions. The dedicated task of the facilitator is to keep the process on track. When an individual from within the organization directs the planning process, there is always the risk that he or she may be sidetracked by the demands of a daily routine.

Excerpted from Driving Strategic Planning: A Nonprofit Executive's Guide *by Deborah L. Kocsis and Susan A. Waechter. BoardSource, 2003. Since this book was published, Cornerstone Consulting Associates, LLC, has moved to Midland, Michigan. Deborah L. Kocsis is now the director of volunteer services for Hospice of Central Ohio.*

3

Changing Our Mindset

CARL BROOKS
President and CEO
The Executive Leadership Council
Washington, DC

Over the last five years, The Executive Leadership Council™ and its charitable arm, The Executive Leadership Foundation™, have taken the commitment to build a pipeline of African American corporate leadership to a higher level. We have seen our organization grow from 19 members in 1986 to nearly 400 members with a diversity of operational experience, industries, corporate affiliations, and global business acumen. Our boards feature some of the most experienced, savvy, and talented senior African American executives in corporate America today. We have let one simple question guide our actions: How do we leverage our unique experience to make the greatest positive impact on our membership and corporate America?

A transition in thinking

In order to address that question, we convened a strategic retreat of executives and board members with expertise in long-term planning and implementation. The honest, open dialogue allowed us to examine our current state and to establish benchmarks for the future that would enhance all of our constituents and ensure a robust future. We followed that up with a strategic financial retreat to ensure that resources were identified to support the robust strategic plan.

A key step in our evolution was the transition from thinking of our organization as simply a membership organization to thinking of it as a unique brand that represented the most dynamic senior African American business executives and their commitment to supporting diversity in the workforce. Given our unique position within the African American community and within corporate America, this change in mindset allowed us to critically examine our programs and make necessary changes to ensure our brand longevity and program quality.

Taking the lead

One of the first strategic decisions was to leverage our position as a repository of research on senior African Americans in corporate America. There are no other organizations that have established themselves as sources of comprehensive research or that could serve as the leading authority on the subject. Our board felt that this was where we could provide a value-added benefit to our members and their companies. By giving them access to this research and helping them utilize it, we hoped to serve as a catalyst to help them create programs to cultivate, develop, and motivate future generations of African American corporate leaders. The outcome of this strategic thinking was the Institute for Leadership Development and Research, established with a founding sponsorship of more than $2.1 million by BP, a global energy supplier. The Institute has already begun to produce high-quality research and developmental programs. The senior executives and "high potentials" who have participated have given the Institute outstanding marks, as have its founding sponsor, Claremont Graduate University (an independent program evaluator), and its corporate sponsors, including AT&T, Moody's, and The Coca-Cola Company.

Building bridges

Another strategy involved seeking partners to work with on significant issues. With workforce diversity becoming a cornerstone of the corporate environment, we believed it was critical to build bridges with organizations whose philosophies and approaches to diversity leadership complemented our own. We did not want to marginalize our voice as simply the African American organization for diversity but to evolve into a globally recognized diversity authority. One issue has involved increasing the numbers of minorities and women on corporate boards. Our board understood the impact minority and female representatives can have on the alignment of strategic plans with diversity plans, and the importance of focusing corporations on issues of succession planning; supplier diversity; and minority training, development, and retention. That is why The Executive Leadership Council teamed up with Catalyst and the Hispanic Association on Corporate Responsibility to form the Alliance for Board Diversity. The Alliance has produced a census of women and minorities on Fortune 100 corporate boards and continues to be an invaluable resource to companies looking for qualified women and minority board applicants.

Our next move was to join forces with the National Association of Investment Companies and the New America Alliance as part of their joint effort called The Marathon Club. The rationale was to help create and maintain real wealth within our community. Such an effort requires the cooperation of individuals with capital to invest and experienced leaders with the entrepreneurial maturity to make it happen. Through this partnership, we have created an environment conducive to capital investment, corporate board leadership, and economic development opportunities in the African American and Latino communities.

Establishing relationships

Finally, to ensure the long-term stability and growth of The Executive Leadership Council, we needed to establish stronger relationships with chief executives and senior corporate executives. One way we do this is through our CEO Diversity Summit sponsored by GE. Now in its sixth year, the Summit serves as a way to link chief executives and senior African American executives of Fortune 500 companies in peer-to-peer discussions on best diversity practices. Offering access to other chief executives is a powerful tool in forging strong relationships within our member companies. It helps them to understand our mission and vision and illustrates the power of inclusive leadership. Chief executives that participate in Council activities are more inclined to invest long-term support in our programs and initiatives.

With the commitment of an enlightened board of directors, we will continue to leverage our relationships with progressive chief executives, Fortune 500 companies, and business organizations to ensure that talented senior executives are prepared for the challenges of a competitive global economy.

Reprinted from Board Member®, *Volume 15, Number 2, March/April 2006.*

CULTURE OF INQUIRY [4]

Exceptional boards institutionalize a culture of inquiry, mutual respect, and constructive debate that lead to sound and shared decision making.

DIMENSIONS

- **INFORMATION** Exceptional boards are informed boards. They seek multiple sources of information by requiring the chief executive to provide a variety of perspectives that present a well-rounded picture of the issue at hand. They do this to prepare for robust and meaningful board discussions and to ensure healthy debate in the boardroom.

- **CULTURE** Exceptional boards engage in thoughtful deliberations. Their members respectfully listen to, acknowledge, and solicit different points of view. They challenge assumptions, conclusions, and each other to make the best decisions for the organization. They are attentive to group dynamics and distribute leadership across the board.

CURIOUS BOARDS

NANCY AXELROD
Principal
NonProfit Leadership Services
Washington, DC

I've always been fascinated by the paradox that a gathering of talented, productive individuals doesn't always result in a talented, productive group. If one hopes to build an exceptional board, one surely needs to start by attracting members with a variety of strengths and abilities. But what's the best way to ensure that these stellar individuals will meld into a brighter constellation?

My three decades of experience as a board anthropologist have taught me that building a strong, positive board culture that transcends any individual or group of individuals is an ongoing challenge. Like all cultures, a board's norms of behavior get passed from one generation of members to the next. Certain practices become so ingrained in group behavior that they occur almost without anyone being conscious of them. The trick is to intentionally instill systems and practices that enhance the board's effectiveness and performance.

I have had ample opportunity to observe individuals who have good group-process skills, the capacity to engage every board member, a sense of curiosity, and the ability to learn and listen "athletically." Regrettably, I've witnessed other board members with ideological rigidity, a fear of inviting views that don't mesh with those of the inner circle, and behavioral patterns that inhibit rich debate and shut down exploratory conversations about how best to advance the mission. It is difficult for a group to generate new, often superior, solutions to its problems until it considers views that may be different from its own. It is the very act of asking questions and engaging in conversation with those who think differently that produces new ideas.

If you've ever had your thinking challenged and been forced to defend or abandon your ideas, you know that this questioning, this sort of curiosity, can be uncomfortable. But a common ingredient of a high-functioning board is the presence of individual members who regularly turn to inquiry over advocacy, especially on matters that are not as clear-cut as other board business that can be tackled in a more perfunctory manner.

Developing a culture of inquiry

Is a culture of inquiry something that any board can develop? Yes, but not overnight. Is it worth the effort? The costs of not doing so can be high. Boards that cannot engage in candid discussions of complex issues unwittingly encourage their members to suppress or channel dissent in destructive ways. Conversely, board members as well as chief executives who understand that dissent does not equal disloyalty and that consensus does not equal unanimity have a greater appetite for these kinds of conversations. Boards that foster a culture of inquiry are not afraid to question complex, controversial, or ambiguous matters or look at issues from all sides. Inviting smart people to do this not only can make a difference to the quality of the outcome but also can make board service more interesting and gratifying. These boards make better decisions because members are better informed as a result of robust discussions in which multiple ideas are vetted. There is less rubber-stamping on such boards. Board members take full ownership of decisions — because everyone's engaged, there's less need to revisit previous decisions, and meetings become more productive.

Does this sound good to you? Does it sound like your board? If you're interested in building this kind of board culture, read on.

Getting started

It is almost impossible to maintain a culture of inquiry if the chief executive and the board chair do not embrace it. When they serve as advocates and role models, they often invest time in building trust, followed closely by three other practices and behaviors — information sharing, generative thinking, and productive meetings.

Trust
The regular turnover on most boards continually tests board culture and group dynamics. As a result, it can be a challenge to create a culture of trust, loyalty, and mutual respect that survives the flux of rotating membership. Here are some key steps you can take to get started:

- Provide social forums for individual board members to get to know each other and the chief executive.
- Make sure everyone has easy access to the organization's documents.
- Make processes transparent.
- Permit individuals to express dissenting views, and, if necessary, coach them on doing it in a constructive way.
- Distribute leadership across the board.
- Do regular board self-assessments.
- Provide opportunities to share accomplishments as well as concerns with the chief executive through ongoing communications, annual performance assessments, and executive sessions.

When there's trust, board members are comfortable sharing different points of view and feel respected by other board members who are listening and considering their comments. Members are able to argue without it being perceived as a personal attack by other members.

Information sharing
Chief executives who regularly distribute relevant and timely articles to their board members keep them informed about what's happening in their sector. Some also invite guest speakers to meetings to provide continuing education about topics related to the organization's mission, programs, and community.

While you're going to external sources for information, don't forget to mine the rich experiences of your own board members. You may be surprised and delighted by the precious social, political, and intellectual capital that your board members have been withholding because the culture didn't prompt them to share it.

Access to useful information is necessary so members can be informed and then engage in lively and challenging discussions. There's nothing like having to defend your point of view to make you consider all sides of it. Such discussions help everyone improve the quality of thinking and the ultimate decisions.

Generative thinking
In their book *Governance as Leadership,* Chait, Ryan, and Taylor highlight the value of generative thinking as a means of producing solutions based on deliberation and analysis — not on gut feelings or personal preferences. It is not realistic or productive to enlist this practice at every board meeting. This kind of approach is especially suited to embryonic, high-stakes issues that have not yet been clearly framed. While generative thinking is an enabler for a culture of inquiry, it can be noisy, scary, and fast. People talk. They challenge. They build on the ideas of others. They frame and reframe situations to think about them in new ways. But it's not just about the solution; it's about making sure they've identified the right problem — possibly something quite different than what they first thought it was.

To stimulate the sharing of different points of view, start slowly, perhaps by designating someone to play the role of devil's advocate. This is one of the most useful tools I've witnessed for pushing people to examine traditional thinking and question assumptions. The devil's advocate role should alternate among different board members, which is why it's important to recruit members who bring candor and reflection to their board roles.

Another trick suggested by Chait and his colleagues to stimulate generative thinking is to begin meetings by asking open-ended questions: What's the biggest gap between what the organization claims it is and what it actually is? What three short phrases best characterize this organization? What do you hope will be most strikingly different about this organization in five years? The discussions that result will help everyone begin to frame issues in new ways.

Well-attended, well-run meetings

Once you've gathered together your board of talented, trustworthy generative thinkers, you need to ensure that their time together is spent productively. Since the tone at the top will influence whether a culture of inquiry will flourish, the chief executive's and chair's roles are critical variables.

Ideally, the chief executive is secure in inviting a range of views, and the chair possesses the skills to manage group dynamics, facilitate discussions, and encourage those not participating to join in and share their perspectives. Together, the chief executive and chair can carry out their roles as the "chief board development officers" by monitoring as well as supporting the culture. Is everyone's voice being heard? Are people listening? Is the atmosphere one where people feel "safe" and comfortable sharing unpopular ideas and questions? Is there an agenda, and does it provide time to focus on what's important? It takes a secure (and courageous) chief executive and chair to keep an eye on all of these elements while being on the lookout for personal agendas or evidence of the Abilene paradox (groupthink resulting in bad decisions based on misinformation).

Since the success of the board will be influenced by the chair's ability to facilitate group interaction, it is important to look for this skill set in officer succession planning. When these qualities are not present in the chair (and when a board agenda item cries out for generative thinking), consider asking another more skilled board member to facilitate the board discussion or bringing in an outside facilitator.

Becoming exceptional

Developing a culture of inquiry where it is not a regular part of the way the board operates won't be easy. Rich debate, hard questions, and seemingly contentious discussions make things more complicated. The absence of a culture of inquiry can lead to groupthink, questionable decisions with unfortunate consequences, and dysfunctional group dynamics. Only when board members are provided with the tools to make the whole greater than the sum of its parts can boards become the exceptional source of collective wisdom that they were originally intended to be.

Reprinted from Board Member®, *Volume 15, Number 3, May/June 2006.*

THE FIVE DYSFUNCTIONS OF A TEAM

1. The first dysfunction is an **absence of trust** among team members. Essentially, this stems from their unwillingness to be vulnerable within the group. Team members who are not genuinely open with one another about their mistakes and weaknesses make it impossible to build a foundation for trust.

2. This failure to build trust is damaging because it sets the tone for the second dysfunction: **fear of conflict.** Teams that lack trust are incapable of engaging in unfiltered and passionate debate of ideas. Instead, they resort to veiled discussions and guarded comments.

3. A lack of healthy conflict is a problem because it ensures the third dysfunction of a team: **lack of commitment.** Without having aired their opinions in the course of passionate and open debate, team members rarely, if ever, buy in and commit to decisions, though they may feign agreement during meetings.

4. Because of this lack of real commitment and buy-in, team members develop an **avoidance of accountability,** the fourth dysfunction. Without committing to a clear plan of action, even the most focused and driven people often hesitate to call their peers on actions and behaviors that seem counterproductive to the good of the team.

5. Failure to hold one another accountable creates an environment where the fifth dysfunction can thrive. **Inattention to results** occurs when team members put their individual needs (such as ego, career development, or recognition) or even the needs of their divisions above the collective goals of the team.

Excerpted from The Five Dysfunctions of a Team *by Patrick Lencioni. Jossey-Bass, 2002.*

4

Rattle Your Board

SANDRA R. HUGHES
Senior Governance
Consultant
BoardSource

Ask a room full of board members to list what's wrong with their board and you may be met with blank stares and awkward silence. No one wants to be the first to admit they may not be doing the best possible job or to point out someone else's flaws.

Instead, ask the board "What would this board be like if your mother were chair?" Response — laughter. Followed by "We'd have great snacks at every meeting," "Meetings would be short!" and "Everyone would pay attention or else." At first these answers may seem irrelevant, but would your mother's instincts be wrong? Ask the group to examine why your mother would do those things at a board meeting and whether they would be effective methods of getting your board into shape.

Questions like that, and 39 others included here, can be excellent catalysts for important conversations that your board, staff, committee, or other group can have. These questions enable participants to step back and gain valuable perspective on the situation at hand. A conversation sparked by these questions can help a board tackle a serious problem while removing some of the personal tension and baggage that can accompany board or group dynamic issues. These questions focus on problem areas and allow members who may be overwhelmed by the laundry list of problems they think their board has to take them one at a time. Board-rattling questions open a group for discussion in a nonthreatening way, injecting much-needed humor and creativity into complex and difficult situations.

The key to making the most use of these questions is to carefully examine the answers and then ask the natural follow-up questions. For example, if a group is talking about what kind of vehicle its board is, and the answer is "an Edsel" or "a speeding freight train that goes so fast there's no time to look around or see where we're going" or "a BMW with a VW engine," ask why? What is wrong with that description, and what is right with it? Once you have a clear picture of what your current situation is, figure out what you aspire to be. What kind of vehicle do you want to be? Why? What are the implications? How can you trade up for a better model? Using these kind of metaphors can be a tremendously useful and a pretty fun way to assess your board and plan for the future.

1. What would your board be like if your mother were the chair?
2. What intangible benefit makes your service as a board member worthwhile?
3. What games do you, as a board member, have to play to get on the right side of those in power?
4. What are the core beliefs? What constitutes a sin?
5. If you could create a new, unique position for yourself on the board, what would it be?
6. What committee do you find to be irrational, deranged, and in need of intensive therapy?
7. What would your organization's epitaph be if it went under tomorrow?
8. What is the most likely reason someone would want to join your board? What is the most likely reason someone would leave it?
9. What would be the top 10 questions customers, members, or suppliers would ask about your board?
10. Is your board a Ferrari, a Ford Taurus, an SUV, or a VW Bug?

11. What is the worst major decision your board has made in recent years? How did that decision get made?

12. What current governance fad has your board adopted that is driving you crazy?

13. Is your board trying to rob you of your individuality?

14. What false or outdated assumptions do board members operate under at the board table?

15. If Hollywood made a movie based on your board, what would be the plot? Which stars would you cast in the lead roles?

16. If you came up with a brilliant idea, who or what might prevent you from implementing it?

17. If you could trade board skills the way kids swap baseball cards, who on the board or off the board would you trade with and for what skills?

18. What about your work on the board reminds you of what you hated about school?

19. If someone burst into your office and shouted, "I've got good news and bad news about the board," what do you think those two pieces of news might be?

20. If you work with one or two incompetent and/or obnoxious board members, how do they manage to keep their seats on the board?

21. What would your board be like if you had never been a member?

22. At a typical board meeting, which of the following takes up most of your time?
    a. Dealing with difficult people on the board
    b. Coming up with productive ideas
    c. Accomplishing little
    d. Using your skills to achieve objectives

23. If you were to be asked to leave the board, what would be the most likely reason?

24. Which of these concepts — teamwork, learning organization, continuous improvement, leadership, or quality — is the biggest joke within your board?

25. What proverb captures the essence of your board?

26. How would Roger Ebert review your board's performance?

27. What would appear bizarre, shocking, or amazing to a Martian visiting your boardroom?

28. What would happen if your board instituted a one-year ban on meetings?

29. What's your idea of a utopian boardroom?

30. Who would be able to solve your most stubborn board structure or operating problem: a master psychologist, a venture capitalist, or an enforcer from the mob?

31. You've just received $100 million to help the organization grow and prosper. How would the board allocate it?

32. What are the top five excuses or reasons board members give for missing a meeting?

33. Why and when do other board members and/or staff make you feel that the information you need to carry out your duties as a board member is "top secret" and you're a "poor security risk"?

34. What incredible invention would make your role as a board member much easier and you much more productive?

35. What unwritten rules on the board make it difficult to get things done quickly, efficiently, or profitably?

36. If your board worked in a big glass fishbowl, what might you all do differently?

37. What barnyard animal would you choose as your team or organizational symbol?

38. You're the board weatherperson; what's your forecast for the board using meteorological terms?

39. If you could forge an alliance with any organization in the world to obtain a needed resource, which one would it be?

40. What particular accomplishment or failure might cause you or your board to make headlines in *Business Week* magazine?

Adapted from 75 Cage-Rattling Questions to Change the Way You Work *by Dick Whitney and Melissa Giovagnoli. McGraw-Hill, 1997.*

Reprinted from Board Member®, *Volume 9, Number 6, June 2000.*

Since this article appeared in Board Member®, *Sandra R. Hughes has become president and CEO of Hughes Consulting Group, Inc.*

A Tradition of Dialogue

LEWIS M. GEDANSKY, PhD
Director, Governance and
Executive Programs
Project Management Institute
Newtown Square, PA

The Project Management Institute (PMI) is a global professional membership association with more than 200,000 members in 155 countries. Because the organization is growing more than 20 percent annually, board members see many changes during their one or two consecutive three-year terms, as they and the organization strive to meet the needs of a diverse customer base spread across multiple market segments. The elected volunteer board of directors of PMI is internationally diverse and flourishes during board meetings because of three key elements:

- A process of maximizing the informal/discussion portions of the meeting and minimizing the actual formal/voting portions
- Advance distribution and full disclosure of meeting agenda topics with all relevant background material for understanding and inquiry prior to the meeting
- Simple mechanisms allowing everyone to have the opportunity to ask questions and participate fully in discussions during the meeting

Maximizing discussion time; minimizing voting time

Having been on the staff of PMI for almost nine years in a variety of positions, I am reminded easily at each board meeting how our board continues to advance its professionalism and performance through the maturation of its practices and procedures. In fact, a PMI board has never reversed a major decision of a previous board because of a tradition of extensive dialogue (sometimes over many years), attainment of the views of other stakeholders, and concurrence, most of the time, on the wording of any motion prior to the formal voting session. That tradition has been improved by a redistribution of the meeting time to mostly informal sessions to discuss topics on the agenda and then into a formal session for the actual voting on any motions planned for the meeting. This approach is aided by written board procedures, i.e., Rules of the Board (available on PMI's Web site), that require distribution of the board meeting agenda, accompanying reading material, and any planned motion at least 15 days prior to the meeting. Board members are expected to be knowledgeable about the agenda material when they arrive at the meeting.

By discussing all relevant material and any planned motion during informal sessions, agreements and disagreements are handled more easily, with most issues being resolved prior to the voting portion of the meeting. For multiday board meetings, this approach is aided by the opportunity for overnight lobbying, additional personal thinking, and, if needed, more informal discussion prior to the vote.

Handling routine matters in a routine manner

Dorothy Hamilton, PMI manager, governance and executive administration, has been instrumental in implementing many of the improvements. She observed, "The PMI board has been able to gain more time for informal discussions about agenda topics by distribution of more routine updates through the Calendar for Receipt and by handling votes on more routine matters through advance distribution of the Consent Calendar for Approval." The Calendar for Receipt contains material that the board should read, but which does not warrant board discussion time. Similarly, the Consent Calendar for Approval contains formal motions, which also generally do not require board discussion time. Such items typically include committee appointments, minor adjustments to the Rules of the Board, and/or modest adjustments to committee charters. However, if any board member feels any topic in the Calendar for Receipt or Consent Calendar for Approval requires clarification and/or board discussion time, that member is asked to resolve the matter prior to the meeting. If necessary, contingency time on the agenda can be devoted to the topic. Once again, this approach allows full discussion, but only when warranted, saving precious board discussion time for more important topics.

Disclosing agenda topics in the advance reading material

Little time is spent during board meetings on reviewing the history of any agenda topic or handling surprises because the established agenda topic template requires extensive disclosure about the topic in the advance reading material, including

- identification and draft wording of any motion (and the required number of votes for approval)
- background
- positions found in PMI's governing documents and positions the board has taken on the topic in previous meetings
- market information and market research
- potential risks associated with acting or not acting
- alternative decisions or actions
- copies of other relevant material

In this way, all board members, veteran and new, have an opportunity to become well versed about the topic. The advance distribution also supports additional exchanges of information prior to the meeting. The discussion during the meeting is done in a way that allows the time and opportunity for all board members to be fully engaged in the topic. Rather than presenting all the information in the advance reading material, the agenda topic leader highlights major elements and devotes the majority of agenda time to questions, comments, and discussion prior to resolution (including the final wording of a motion, if relevant). While the agenda topic leader facilitates the discussion, another board member keeps a running list of board members who wish to speak on the topic. In that way, no one has to focus on getting the attention of the discussion leader and thinking about what they want to say, but instead can listen to the discussion. Through this mechanism, everyone gets time to speak (one or more times) in a fair manner and the topic leader does not get distracted. When done, the sense of the group is tested about any planned motion.

Thus, through a series of procedures and behaviors, PMI board members continue to advance the "culture of inquiry" as a critical element of board maturity so they can focus their attention on knowledge-based decision making to enable the achievement of the PMI strategic plan.

Reprinted from Board Member®, *Volume 15, Number 3, May/June 2006.*

5

INDEPENDENT-MINDEDNESS [5]

Exceptional boards are independent-minded. When making decisions, board members put the interests of the organization above all else.

DIMENSIONS

- **DEBATE** Exceptional boards do not allow their votes to be unduly influenced by loyalty to the chief executive or by seniority, position, or reputation of fellow board members, staff, or donors. Instead, they rely on open debate to uncover all facets of an issue and then distill their perspectives into autonomous and informed decisions.

- **CONFLICT OF INTEREST** To ensure that the organization's best interests come first, exceptional boards establish and rigorously adhere to conflict-of-interest policies that include guidelines for disclosure, review, and recusal. Board members sign conflict-of-interest statements annually and require other individuals with decision-making power to do so as well.

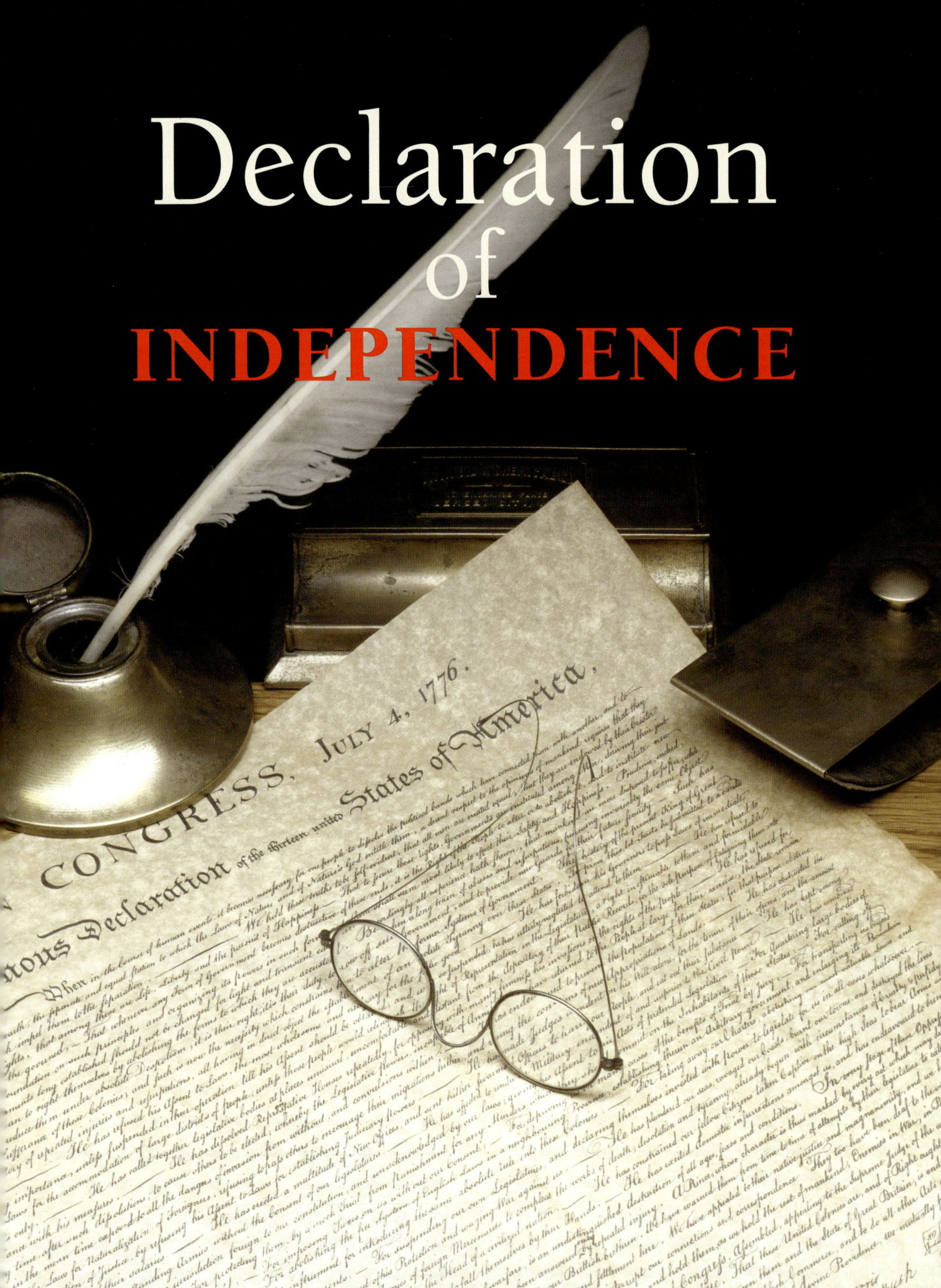

MAUREEN K. ROBINSON
Consultant
Bethesda, MD

Independent-mindedness is fundamentally about making decisions free of undue influence. In the boardroom, it requires a measure of detachment that seems to contradict the energetic embracing of mission at the heart of board service and a periodic distancing from the executive and other influential players that can easily feel ungrateful or untrusting. It has to feel helpful rather than merely cranky and be exerted steadily rather than in fits and starts. Independent-mindedness is a board quality that depends heavily on the ability of individual board members to appreciate its value and find constructive ways to exercise it.

The greatest challenge in building an independent board is getting all the elements of good governance to come together — a sturdy framework of policy and practice; a smart, secure executive; enough collective time together to build experience and a decent culture; and finally, a strong majority of individual board members who have overcome their hodgepodge of experience, style, and attention spans to work together as a unit. Easier said than done.

Policy and practice

Good governance is not achieved through mind reading. Nuance may be useful, but, generally, subtlety is not. The natural turnover that is part and parcel of board life requires that an organization take the time to articulate its values and be frank about what constitutes acceptable performance. Why leave these matters to the imagination or rely solely on good will or good sense to maintain the effectiveness of the board and its capacity to be independent-minded? A clear conflict-of-interest policy with sensible mechanisms for complying with it does not imply a lack of faith in board members' ability to detect and avoid these situations on their own. Rather, it expresses a common understanding of what will put a board member in conflict with the interests of the organization and provides board members, the board, and the organization with a way to deal with these moments consistently and in a straightforward, open, and unembarrassed way.

The same could be said of values statements and the agreements board members reach about their own behavior. An association board, whose members could be characterized more for their clout than their deference, compiled a list of boardroom values that went beyond important but expected concepts, such as mutual respect and integrity, to include less expected, but probably more necessary, behaviors for the group, such as listening and the pledge to keep issues in the room and on the table. How much easier it is to agree as a board to park bad habits, personal interests, and hobby horses at the door than to correct misguided enthusiasm or blind spots instance by painful instance.

Similarly, what makes more sense for the organization and the board — to look at the executive's performance in a thoughtful and consistent way each year or to put a process in place only when the relationship is under stress? Someday, we will routinely connect evaluation with learning instead of judgment and punishment. On that day, the annual evaluation of the executive director will be seen as the best way to strengthen everyone's performance rather than an exercise in re-assurance or the run up to farewell.

Being independent-minded and having both the policies and practices that support it clearly in place is not being rigid and bureaucratic but sensible.

Culture

Independent-mindedness is like regular exercise, part of a healthy board lifestyle; the temptation to slough off should be gently resisted. It is a challenge to chair a board or committee and make it your job to insist on preparation and invite healthy debate. It's tough to look at a budget and express doubt that, given past performance, the projected income is realistic. Or to look at the cost of a project and wonder if the money is well spent. Even constructive criticism may initially be interpreted as imputing that someone's favorite child is homely.

It is easier to go with the flow, particularly when the flow is swift and positive and deliberation might slow it down. I know of a terrific organization with an energetic and charismatic executive who produced outstanding results year after year. But a moment came when the executive found it harder and harder to pull rabbits out of the hat and even more difficult to admit this to his admiring board. The board, not wanting to appear to doubt the executive's abilities, averted its gaze. Admiration, sympathy, gratitude, and loyalty — all good sentiments in and of themselves — conspired in the boardroom to undo an organization.

Nothing kills independent-mindedness more quickly than prizing comfort over stewardship or mistaking timidity for politeness. This is not a culture in which good governance can thrive. Board chairs and executives recognize such behavior and discourage it. Instead, they invite good questions, play devil's advocate, and have the stamina to withstand a few knocks along the way. The chair in particular should know the difference and strike a balance between acceptance that masks passivity as well as healthy disagreement at risk of becoming a free-for-all.

Independent-mindedness also requires critical mass. If only one or two members of the board have it in them to bring this quality to the boardroom, it is much harder for the board as a whole to enjoy it. An obligation exists among all board members to be attentive and engaged rather than diffident and disconnected. To lead by example is great, but you need to look back and see some followers for the board, as the sum of its parts, to achieve independent-mindedness.

A relationship, not a romance

Perhaps the toughest aspect of being independent-minded is separating the emotional content of the board's relationship to the executive and other players in the organization — whether a founder, influential board members, or long-tenured program staff or volunteers — from the work itself. Sometimes the emotion is gratitude and admiration; sometimes it is anxiety; and, if we are honest, sometimes it is a fear that rocking the boat might require picking up an oar. Nevertheless, it is the board's role to step back periodically and provide a deliberately neutral perspective.

There are many mechanisms available to encourage and support the positive neutrality that ensures that missions are met and people are served. None requires that boards sacrifice the powerful emotions that both reward and complicate the assignment: goals that board and staff believe in; evaluations of results that are genuinely thoughtful and rigorous; an evaluation process for the executive that is respectful but thorough; regular board self-assessment; and the habit of holding individual members accountable, not just for showing up but for the quality of their participation. This last is a particularly difficult but essential step toward independent-mindedness. A board is too easily captive to its least-effective members and must demonstrate the courage of its convictions in asking that all members do their part.

BoardSource characterizes boards that are independent-minded as exceptional. While this is undoubtedly true, it is not an achievement out of reach for most boards and well worth extolling. Although our missions are often difficult and sometimes quixotic, they are rarely romantic or inconsequential.

Independent-minded boards build relationships with the mission, the work, and the people involved that are resilient and durable, graceful, and deeply satisfying.

Reprinted from Board Member®, *Volume 16, Number 2, March/April 2007.*

Conflicts of Interest: Avoiding the Bad and Managing the Good

Nonprofits seek active and engaged individuals to serve on their boards because they bring expertise, talents, and a commitment to the communities served by the organization. Such individuals often face challenges in carrying out their board responsibilities; the number and breadth of associations they have make it likely that they will face situations that involve multiple loyalties. Making unbiased, independent decisions on behalf of a nonprofit can be difficult when a colleague, a friend, a family member, or a business relationship may be affected by, or benefit from, those decisions.

Multiple loyalties can create conflicts of interest. In nonprofits, conflicts of interest occur when the financial or personal interests of board members are, or may appear to be, inconsistent with the interests of the nonprofit.

These situations arise, for example, when a nonprofit wants to hire a board member's company to provide advice or lease space in an office building owned by the family of a board member.

In some cases, conflict-of-interest transactions violate the law; in other situations, they work to a nonprofit's advantage. Regardless of intention or result, however, nonprofits, their boards, and their managers must act very carefully when dealing with transactions that are, or may appear to be, inconsistent with a nonprofit's interest for the following reasons:

- First, conflict-of-interest transactions can create substantial legal liability, especially if they violate the self-dealing prohibitions under the federal tax laws. In those situations, board members and nonprofit managers can be personally liable because they engaged in the transactions, approved them, or both.

- Second, conflicts of interest carry very real risks of negative public perception. As charitable institutions provided with special tax status, nonprofits are expected to serve the public trust. When they engage in improper transactions — or those that give the appearance of impropriety — the damage can extend beyond their good name and reputation to the charitable sector as a whole.

- Lastly, conflicts can compromise the decision-making process, preventing board members and managers from having open and candid discussions and, in some cases, from acting in the best interests of the nonprofit.

The following discussion will guide board members and managers in defining conflicts of interest, identifying which transactions are absolutely prohibited and which are permissible if properly handled, and developing a conflict-of-interest policy that protects foundations, board members, and managers by taking self-interest out of the decision-making process.

For nonprofits, the bottom line is this: Conflicts of interest should either be avoided or managed in such a way that the organization and its board and managers are protected from liability or unwelcome publicity. By answering the following five questions and by following the processes recommended here, nonprofits can minimize legal risks; protect themselves and their board members and managers against bad publicity; and most of all, ensure the integrity of their decision-making process. The five questions are

1. Is this transaction a conflict of interest or could it be perceived as such by others?

2. Is it prohibited by the self-dealing rules under the Internal Revenue Code?

3. Even if the transaction is not prohibited by the self-dealing rules, is it unfair to the nonprofit? i.e., does it improperly benefit another person or organization?

4. Does the transaction create an appearance problem? How would it look on the front page of tomorrow's newspaper or to the organization's founders?

5. Has the organization followed its conflict-of-interest policy and documented that fact?

Is this a conflict of interest?

The starting point for managing conflicts of interest is to know when they exist.

A conflict of interest arises whenever the "financial or personal interests" of a board member or manager are, or appear to be, inconsistent or at odds with the interests of the organization.

Most nonprofit conflicts of interest arise in the context of proposed transactions with parties that fall in the following general categories:

REPORTING A CONFLICT OF INTEREST

A conflict of interest exists when a board member, officer, or management employee has a personal interest that is in conflict with the interests of the organization, such that he or she may be influenced by this personal interest when making a decision for the organization. When a conflict occurs, to whom should it be reported?

This key question has two parts: First, who should be responsible for collecting, reading, and retaining board and staff disclosure statements? Second, if a conflict arises between the filing of annual disclosure statements, how and to whom should this conflict be reported?

A good option is a committee of the board — either one that is specifically charged with dealing with conflicts, or a more general governance committee, which also may be responsible for the organization's bylaws and other governance matters. The best approach will depend on the overall size and structure of the organization, but it is a good idea for the responsible group or committee to involve the board chair in handling reported conflicts. Some boards designate a compliance officer (or conflicts officer) who both monitors disclosure statements and serves as the point person when interim conflicts arise. The compliance officer may be the chair of the group or committee charged with handling conflicts.

The compliance officer should collect disclosure statements from new board members and staff who are covered by the policy, and should ensure that statements of current board and staff members are updated annually and in between annual filings, if significant organizational changes occur that pose a possibility of a conflict. In large organizations, a lawyer in the counsel's office may handle the collection of statements from new individuals, as well as other compliance responsibilities.

If an individual has been designated to receive reports of conflicts in the first instance, he or she can then refer the issue to a governance committee, an executive committee, an audit committee, or the full board. Alternatively, there may be a board committee that has decision-making authority over the substantive matter in question.

Adapted from Managing Conflicts of Interest, Second Edition, *by Daniel L. Kurtz and Sarah E. Paul. BoardSource, 2006.*

1. Board members and managers
2. Family members of board members and managers
3. Organizations in which board members, managers, and/or their family members have a significant financial relationship
4. Organizations in which a board member, manager, and/or family member is an officer, director, trustee, or employee

Applying those categories, nonprofits can find themselves facing conflicts of interest when they propose to take actions such as engaging a board member's law firm for professional services, hiring the president's spouse as a program officer, selling property to a board member's grandchild, or making grants to a charity run by a board member's child.

Has the organization followed its conflict-of-interest policies and processes?

For many nonprofits, conflicts of interest can be unavoidable. To ensure that the organization, its board, and its managers do not engage in illegal or risky decisions, the board should

1. Adopt a written conflict-of-interest policy, which includes, at a minimum, the following provisions:

    - A statement of who the policy applies to (typically board members and managers)

    - A definition of what constitutes a conflict of interest (including which family members and affiliated entities are encompassed within the policy; some extended family relationships may be too remote to raise conflict issues)

    - A requirement that parties covered by the policy disclose any conflict to the board (or a designated board committee) in advance and leave the room during the board's discussion and decision

    - A prohibition against any attempt by a board member or manager with a conflict to influence the decision (i.e., a board member with a conflict may not lobby other board members)

    - A requirement that the existence and resolution of the conflict be documented in the organization's records (typically the minutes of the meeting when the transaction was considered)

    - A requirement that the organization consult with its tax advisor as appropriate to ensure that the proposed transaction does not constitute an act of self-dealing

2. Require board members and managers to fill out annual disclosure forms that list their affiliations and the names of businesses in which they have a significant ownership interest and, to the extent known, those of family members that are covered by the conflict-of-interest policy.

3. Before approving a proposed conflict-of-interest transaction, make sure that all the requirements of the conflict policy have been followed, including the requirement to obtain market data showing that the proposed transaction is reasonable, and then document the basis for the board's action (including reliance on market data) in the minutes.

Even the most comprehensive conflict-of-interest policy cannot cover every conceivable situation where there might be the appearance of a conflict. Accordingly, conflict-of-interest policies should encourage board members and managers to follow the process outlined above any time there might be the appearance or perception of conflict, even if it is not directly covered by the policy.

Adapted from the white paper, Conflict of Interest at Foundations: Avoiding the Bad and Managing the Good. *BoardSource, 2005.*

5

Daring To Innovate

LOWELL NOTEBOOM
Board Chair
The Saint Paul Chamber Orchestra
Saint Paul, MN

The Saint Paul Chamber Orchestra (SPCO) is America's only full-time, salaried, professional chamber orchestra. Now in its 47th year, the SPCO is unique in many respects, including its artistic leadership structure and its approach to governance.

In a field where tradition and resistance to change abound, the SPCO prides itself on being highly innovative. In fact, our new "tradition" is innovation. We have learned that it pays huge dividends, not only with our audiences but also with our musicians, board, and staff. Gone are the days when the standard response to a new idea was, "We never did it that way before." Instead, innovation and new ways of thinking about challenges and addressing them have become central to our mission.

How did we do this? Over the course of 18 months in 2000–2001, our 57 board members, 36 musicians, 34 professional staff, and several community leaders took a fresh look at everything we were doing. Using Jim Collins's approach, we established a clear institutional vision ("Innovative discovery and distinctive experience through the brilliant performance and vigorous advocacy of the chamber orchestra and chamber music repertoire"), identified our values (excellence, innovation, intimacy, and continuity), and established our BHAGs (big, hairy, audacious goals): to be widely recognized as America's chamber orchestra, to be clearly distinctive in artistic profile, and to be the symbol of excellence in the Twin Cities.

Confronting our brutal realities (a Collins imperative) led us to recognize that the SPCO had an artistic competition problem. At home we competed for audience, board members, contributions, press attention, and a place in the community psyche. Around the world we competed for tour opportunities, conductors, guest artists, musicians, composers, recording opportunities, and radio airtime. We asked ourselves: Should we keep doing the same thing, only better? Pretend there was no competition? Treat it as if it were someone else's problem? Or tackle it head on? We chose to tackle it head on.

We decided we wanted everything about the SPCO — performances, musicians, board, and staff — to be much better…to be great. That meant better planning, better artistic performance, better leadership (on stage, in the boardroom, and in our management), better attendance, and better funding. To be innovative and to go from good to great, we needed to make major changes. Here's what we did.

From music director to artistic partners

For all their wonderful attributes and star power, good music directors are hard to find, hard to keep, noncollaborative, usually really great in only one repertoire, and never available full time because they have multiple orchestras in other cities or countries. So we eliminated the position and established two committees to be responsible for everything the music director did except conducting. Each committee is comprised of three musicians and two staff, and all decisions are made by consensus (if they can't agree, a supermajority vote of four is required, but there hasn't been a single vote needed since they started). The Artistic Vision Committee sets artistic direction and policies, plans programs, and chooses guest artists and guest conductors.

The Artistic Personnel Committee is responsible for hiring (auditions), professional feedback, and (in rare instances) intervention. Next, we hired five artistic partners, all wonderful conductors and world-class artists, who committed to be with us for at least three years. Each spends two or three weeks a season with us; brings greatness within a segment of the repertoire; inspires the musicians and audience in unique ways; and brings a level of energy and excitement that has created electricity in the hall and throughout the organization.

From musician employees to musician board members

We invited three musicians onto the board and executive committee, with full voting rights. Other musicians serve on various board committees, where they deal with questions of finance or marketing, and are active in fundraising activities, such as assisting in making calls on donors.

From term limits to continuity and stability

As we implemented our plan, it became apparent that maintaining continuity on the board during this time of dramatic organizational change was vitally important. We already had incredible vitality and engagement, and we wanted to hold onto it. So the board eliminated term limits and established its own tools for accountability. Board members are still elected for three-year terms, but they can be re-elected, provided they remain fully engaged. Annual surveys and evaluations of board members by the governance committee test their commitment and weed out unproductive members.

From powerful executive committee to board engagement

The executive committee had begun to be perceived as a "board within the board," a place where important issues were decided before they came to the full board for "rubber-stamping." So we reduced its size and took away its power to make decisions except in emergencies. Now its sole responsibility is to ensure that issues coming to the board have been carefully prepared, that the right information has been gathered, and that board questions have been anticipated. Changing its role from decision maker to preparer has resulted in greater board engagement, a commitment to using board meetings for in-depth discussions of important issues, and a real sense of ownership of the organization, its mission, and its people.

From traditional bargaining to collaborative contract renewal

In 2003, we took a new approach to developing a contract with the musicians. We utilized a nonconfrontational, facilitated process, with four board members, five musicians, and three senior managers participating in dozens of sessions over a seven-month period, resulting in a contract that tracked closely on the strategic plan. We will do it again in 2007.

From high prices to accessibility and family-friendly pricing

One of the best examples of board engagement came nearly two years ago, when we confronted declining attendance (nearly 20 percent over a five-year period). The board confronted the issue head on, carefully evaluated the options and the risks of lowering ticket prices, and concluded that our commitment to innovation should be our guide. We slashed ticket prices, and the response was overwhelming. Attendance has soared (higher than at any time in the past five years), many concerts are sold out, more neighborhood venues have been created, and editorials in the local press have been enthusiastic. And it all happened because a tradition of innovation had taken hold.

These are only six examples of a culture change that has occurred at the SPCO. It all started with a commitment to innovation and to a collaborative, inclusive form of governance. We are excited about the future.

Reprinted from Board Member®, *Volume 16, Number 2, March/April 2007.*

6

ETHOS OF TRANSPARENCY 6

Exceptional boards promote an ethos of transparency by ensuring that donors, stakeholders, and interested members of the public have access to appropriate and accurate information regarding finances, operations, and results.

DIMENSIONS

- **OUTREACH** To fulfill their accountability to the public, exceptional boards ensure that their organizations disclose appropriate information to stakeholders. They do this by making sure the organization posts key documents, such as the IRS Form 990 and an annual report, on its Web site.

- **OPENNESS** Exceptional boards extend transparency internally by making sure that every board member has equal access to relevant materials when making decisions. They also institute policies to ensure that staff will feel comfortable bringing appropriate matters to their attention.

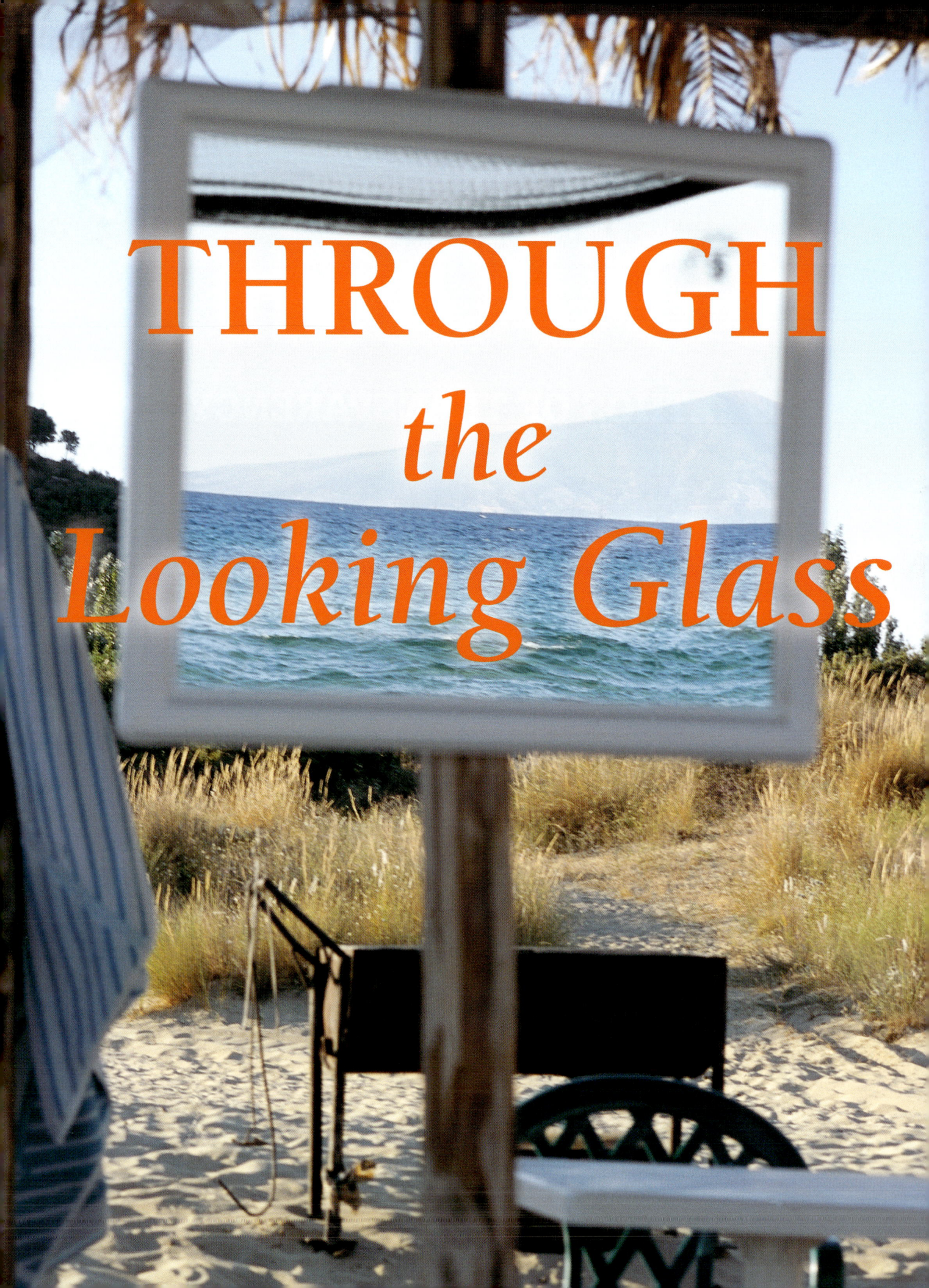

ANNE COHN DONNELLY
Professor
Kellogg School of Management
Northwestern University
Evanston, IL

Given a nonprofit's obligation to serve the public good, one might ask how the public, the government, and other stakeholders know that the mission is being advanced and the public interest is being served. The answer: transparency.

There are various ways an organization can ensure transparency. It can make sure information about the organization's work and actions is clear, accurate, and timely. It can regularly hold a mirror up to its practices and behavior, taking a long, hard look at itself and allowing others to do so.

When the board and the organization's leaders allow others to stare into the looking glass — not just at the successes and progress, but also at the failures and setbacks — confidence and trust in the organization follow. On the heels of trust comes support.

What does transparency look like?

Transparency begins with open communication among board members and between the board and staff. It includes basics, such as all board members having access to the same information when making decisions and staff members having access to information about the organization's business (e.g., board meeting minutes, annual budgets).

Openness continues with external transparency, with being accountable to the public and outside stakeholders, such as donors and clients. This includes disclosure of general information and annual reports, as well as proactive communications of good and bad news.

Let's look at some guidelines for practicing transparency.

Information is disseminated.
Being internally transparent, a chief executive willingly and immediately shares major news, good or bad, with the board. For example, when a donor says yes or no to a significant request, the chief executive e-mails the board immediately. When big changes happen at the organization, key donors and stakeholders are notified quickly. This isn't burdensome when the chief executive and board appropriately define "major" for their organization.

Information is available and up-to-date.
To be externally transparent, an organization's Web site should list board members, staff, program descriptions, and explanations of how to volunteer and make donations. Going one step further, an organization should post its most recent Form 990 and audited financial statements.

Beyond these "quantifiable" indicators of transparency are two "qualitative" tactics that have less to do with documents and more to do with an organization's views about openness and honesty. Both are examples of internal transparency.

Hard questions are asked, and hard truths are spoken.
Trust among players in the organization is such that no one is intimidated when speaking out. Whistleblower policies serve as one way to protect staff and cultivate a sense of trust. Likewise, board members need to be able to

share their concerns. I was involved in determining why a children's museum had fallen on hard times. One board member said, "I took my grandchildren to the museum. We had such a bad time that I would never take them back. But we don't have the kind of board where you can say that at a meeting."

Performance is assessed regularly.
Set aside 10 minutes at the end of every board meeting to discuss how you did and whether you used your time and talent well. Once a year, complete a more directed board assessment and then openly discuss the results. Engage an external facilitator to bring in a fresh, neutral perspective and help guide the board's discussion.

Are there legitimate arguments against transparency?

I often hear the reasons why an organization or board's work isn't as transparent as it might be.

Transparency takes too much time and effort.
True enough. It takes real resources to gather good, thorough information on cash flow, program impact, staff turnover, funding request rejection rates, and overhead rates and then to make the information easily digestible. But the risk of not spending time on transparency is that your stakeholders may be less likely to support your organization because they don't feel they know enough about your good work.

"Too much information" may make staff and volunteers uncomfortable.
While it's easy to share successes, most of us don't want to broadcast our troubles or failures. Why would any chief executive with a sense of self-preservation want to tell the board about struggles managing staff or a looming deficit? Because two (or more) heads are better than one. The board is there to help and offer guidance on difficult issues. It's far better for the chief executive to practice the "doctrine of no surprises" because the level of trust usually goes up when leaders are open about problems. And, together, they can determine how to solve them.

Shouldn't some of what we do be confidential?
Yes. There is certainly information that few, if any, outside the board need to know or even have a right to know. No one outside the board, for example, needs to know the results of a chief executive's performance review and assessments of individual board members. It's perfectly reasonable not to share operating plans and budgets with the public. Prudent judgment and input from the staff and board can help determine what data may be revealed to whom.

Is there a cost to being too transparent?

The costs of not being transparent may be greater than being too open. Without public trust, a nonprofit has little chance of thriving, let alone surviving. Simply put, trust brings support.

A board that is exceptional at living transparently makes sure that the information it shares is given a context and an explanation. Going to a donor and saying "the program you funded failed" is certainly not as useful as saying "the program you funded failed for the following reasons; here is what we learned from the failure and how we will do things differently in the future." Such an explanation is as much a part of being transparent as the description of the failure itself.

The pluses of transparency

While it is easy to enumerate barriers that inhibit boards and their organizations from embracing an ethos of transparency, there are many more reasons to embrace it. In addition to the core value of maintaining public trust, other benefits include

- Donors, board members, and other stakeholders may become active partners in solving problems, thereby strengthening the organization. For example, within hours of being told about a potential and major cash-flow problem, the staff of a national organization had more than a dozen ideas for saving funds, ranging from more careful use of office supplies to each staff person taking one day off without pay every other week.

- The surprise of receiving bad information is greatly diminished. When boards, staff, and donors expect to hear both good and bad news, they are better prepared to respond to bad information. For example, when the chief executive takes the time to provide weekly bulletins to all board members on fundraising efforts — who said yes and no and which requests are still outstanding — board members invariably volunteer to see how they can help with outstanding requests and even the rejections.

- Planning and developing strategy is far easier and more effective when you know what to expect, and better decisions can be made if all the facts and pros and cons are on the table. For example, when two nonprofits planning to share space owned by one of them met, the owner disclosed that the building had not been well maintained and substantial dollars would soon be needed to repair it — dollars that the nonprofit owner did not have. Rather than running the other way, the "tenant" worked to determine how the two organizations together could raise the necessary dollars.

Becoming transparent

Transparency is not easy to achieve and certainly can't be achieved overnight. Younger, smaller, or more nimble organizations may find it easier to move toward transparency. Older, larger, more institutionalized nonprofits may believe that they have much more at stake and may find change harder. Nevertheless, embracing transparency is well worth the effort. A more informed stakeholder base strengthens fundraising, partnerships, and staff and board commitment.

Reprinted from Board Member®, *Volume 16, Number 3, May/June 2007.*

Rocking the Cradle

JULIE S. TYE
President
The Cradle
Evanston, IL

The Cradle, an 84-year-old adoption agency, is a pioneer in a field characterized by secrecy. The Cradle has sat on the same corner of Ridge and Simpson in Evanston, Illinois, since 1923. For many years, fluorescent blue light radiating from the windows of the nursery on the second floor was the only sign that infants were being cared for while adoption plans were being considered. Beyond that, very little was known and understood about what we did, how we did it, or who we did it for.

In 1992, it became apparent that the organization was facing a dire situation. Clients stopped seeking services, and the donor base was shrinking. While a number of factors contributed to the situation, there was no question that lack of transparency was a major one. A new management team was brought in and, together with the board, we embarked on a process of shining light on the organization.

Transparency is inside out

We began by focusing internally, identifying key indicators of our operations and fiercely measuring against them with weekly and monthly metrics. These were reported to the board on a routine basis, which gave the board confidence that the staff was on top of things. We broadened the board's exposure to the staff, assigning managers to various board committees and asking them to work directly with the chairs in achieving the committees' charters. We adopted an attitude of candor in describing the challenges we were facing, and board members became actively and positively engaged in finding solutions to those challenges. For example, we were not achieving desired results in serving the African American community. Board members were creative and helpful in developing more effective strategies to reach out to this community.

We instituted a monthly Activity Update that kept the board informed of progress toward goals, as well as problems that were looming. As a new sense of partnership began to form between the staff and the board, we implemented an aggressive communications strategy with our stakeholders through frequent written and personal communication. Our quarterly newsletter contained articles that made the mission come alive to readers. One donor told us she reads the newsletter aloud to her husband during the evening news! As a result of these activities, our stakeholders became re-engaged in the organization. Lapsed donors began renewing their support, and loyal donors increased theirs. As we described the excellent work that was being done, donors felt a sense of inclusion and pride. We took some risks too, including forming a partnership with Planned Parenthood of Chicago. Our stakeholders considered this a bold initiative and felt they had a hand in making it happen.

Transparency is outside in

The trust that developed between the board and the staff was vital for the next phase of the evolution toward transparency. The staff knew that the historic case for closed adoptions could no longer be made because the adoption process itself was moving toward transparency in the form of full disclosure between birth parents and adoptive families. All of our board members were parents who had adopted under the old rules. We needed to demonstrate that open adoption was effective and that closed adoptions were far from perfect, and we needed to do so without causing our board members to feel that they, as parents, had adopted their own children the wrong way.

Since the organization was becoming comfortable with sharing internal information externally, we decided to do the reverse, too, and allow ourselves to be influenced by what was happening outside The Cradle. We benchmarked our services against those of other reputable adoption agencies, we looked at the research on current adoption practices, we brought in families who experienced the benefits of open adoption, and we listened to birth mothers and adult adopted persons for whom closed adoption had been painful. This education process took three years. At a meeting that coincided with the 75th anniversary of The Cradle, the board formally and unanimously approved a policy of open adoption.

Transparency within the board

Until now, our focus has been on the staff reporting to the board and the board reporting to stakeholders. We are about to add a third leg to this stool.

Board members are the most effective fundraisers, though they rarely relish the role. But, as the saying goes, "you get what you measure." We are about to measure board members' activity in reaching out to donors. Board members will be provided with a "playbook" that contains a "game plan" for a few select prospects with whom the board member is likely to have a relationship. The game plan may include making a phone call, writing a personal note, and/or arranging a lunch — any move that will bring the prospect closer to The Cradle. Board members will be asked to report on their activity on a regular basis. I knew that we were on target when one board member referred to the playbook as a "nag-a-matic."

Keeping it all going

We now face an unexpected dilemma. With measurement and reporting hard-wired into our systems, how can we avoid overwhelming our board and stakeholders? Transparency is not only about providing access to meaningful information; it is about providing information that is also digestible.

We are responding to this dilemma on two fronts. First, we use a balanced scorecard to measure our mission. We believe in Jim Collins's *Good to Great* model and have framed our measurements within his concepts of superior performance, distinctive impact, and lasting endurance. Most of the metrics are quantitative; many are qualitative; all are reportable.

Second, because timing is everything, we sought a way for our board members to get information when they are most receptive to it — just-in-time reporting, so to speak. Believing access to information should be under the control of board members, we will establish a Web site with access initially restricted to board members. It will contain key dashboard metrics, a calendar of meetings, and messages from senior staff.

Transparent organizations are learning organizations

When the Sarbanes-Oxley Act was still just a gleam in a regulator's eye, The Cradle learned that transparency is more than simply complying with reporting requirements. It is an attitude, a vital ingredient for any organization that is committed to improving itself. As one board member put it, "By providing windows for stakeholders to gaze through, we are forced to continually check ourselves in the mirror." While there are many elements that are required for excellence, transparency is one of the most important.

Reprinted from Board Member®, *Volume 16, Number 3, May/June 2007.*

6

To Disclose or Not To Disclose

The more information a nonprofit organization shares, the easier it is for the public to determine whether it is worthy of support. Legally, nonprofits are subject to demonstrate a minimum of transparency, but to exceed that minimum can often determine a nonprofit's reputation and prove beneficial if its practices are ever called into question. At the same time, indiscriminate openness can sometimes backfire. Each nonprofit needs to know where to draw the line between what remains internal confidential information and the public's need to know.

What is transparency?

Transparency refers to the public's right to know how its money is being used; after all, it is the general public that supports nonprofits through direct donations and support via the organization's tax exemption. The public has the right to know whether a nonprofit is well-managed, properly governed, and financially secure; whether it abides by ethical standards and values, obeys the law, and functions in a productive and resourceful manner. By sharing information with its supporters and other stakeholders, the nonprofit can avoid a perceived veil of secrecy and perform its activities in a transparent and open manner.

Why transparency is necessary

Functioning in a transparent manner is the key to earning the public's trust. When an organization loses trust, it also loses its supporters. Without supporters, it is impossible to survive and advance the mission of the organization. Equally, transparency is a tool for accountability. When the board assumes its role as the body accountable for the organization, performance needs to be closely tied to meeting goals. With clear objectives and guidelines within a transparent structure, responsiveness and responsibility work hand in hand.

Public information

There are a few documents that nonprofits are legally obligated to share with the public or their members.

- Form 990 is the number one transparency tool. With some exceptions, every nonprofit with a budget of more than $25,000 must file the form with the IRS and make it available to anyone requesting it. Copies of the forms from the past three years can be requested. One easy way to meet this IRS requirement is to post the form on the nonprofit's own Web site or with GuideStar at www.guidestar.org. Form 990 informs the public about how the nonprofit created revenue, how it spent its money, whether board members were compensated, how much the five highest staff members earned, and various other financial and programmatic details. The organization is able to attach additional descriptions of its activities so that no one is forced to judge it only by trying to interpret figures.

- Forms 1023 and 1024, the tax-exemption application forms, also must be readily available. These forms explain the original purpose of the organization and allow those interested to verify that the primary mandate is still being respected.

- Specific financial documents must be made available to members as state laws specify. Formal membership organizations need to know their state's requirements.

- Board meetings, meeting notices, and minutes must be open or available to the public if the organization is covered by state sunshine laws. Please see www.rcfp.org/tapping/index.cgi.

Private information

A nonprofit is not obligated to share planning documents that allow it to remain competitive, prepare for the future, or simply brainstorm about future possibilities. Confidential material that would jeopardize the reputation or integrity of an individual must also remain undisclosed. The following are instances where information does not need to be shared with the general public.

- The budget is the financial guide for a particular project or an entire organization. As accurate and well calculated as it can be, it still is just a plan. Anything can happen to change that plan. Financial statements demonstrate how an organization's budgetary plans were executed and take the role of serving as indicators of its financial activities.

- Form 990-T clarifies whether an organization was involved in unrelated business activities and paid taxes on that income.

- Executive session minutes are distributed only to board members or anyone else present at a meeting. The discussion of confidential issues is the most common reason to have an executive session.

- Donors have a right to remain anonymous. If a donor requests that his or her name not be disclosed to anyone outside the senior staff and the board, the organization is wise to honor that request. The list of all donors attached to Form 990 is not part of the public disclosure.

- Private addresses of board members should remain private. On the Form 990 it is acceptable to list the organization's address for every board member.

- Personnel files naturally are private files. Even board members normally should have no need to see them.

- Patient and client information should not be shared with outsiders. In the health care field, the Health Insurance Portability and Accountability Act (HIPAA) protects medical records.

And the rest

The law only indicates the minimum requirements for disclosure. Openness about how the board and the organization operate is the easiest way to garner goodwill. Information from audited financial statements to documents outlining organizational and board policies and procedures help eliminate questions and concerns. A climate of secrecy only invites curiosity. The organization's Web site is the most obvious place to introduce an organization to those interested in its activities.

Excerpted from the topic paper, Creating Transparency. *BoardSource, 2006.*

COMPLIANCE WITH INTEGRITY 7

Exceptional boards promote strong ethical values and disciplined compliance by establishing appropriate mechanisms for active oversight.

DIMENSIONS

- **FINANCIAL OVERSIGHT** Exceptional boards ensure that the organization is financially sound and that its assets are well managed by reviewing financial statements, undertaking an annual audit or independent financial review, and making sure internal controls are in place. They use these mechanisms to deepen their understanding of the organization and minimize the risk of waste, fraud, and abuse. To protect the organization's assets, they also ensure that the organization has adequate insurance and contingency plans.

- **LEGAL AND ETHICAL OVERSIGHT** To ensure compliance with legal and regulatory requirements, exceptional boards establish policies, stay abreast of applicable laws, and review key documents. They also articulate an explicit set of ethical standards and make sure these standards are clearly communicated to internal and external stakeholders.

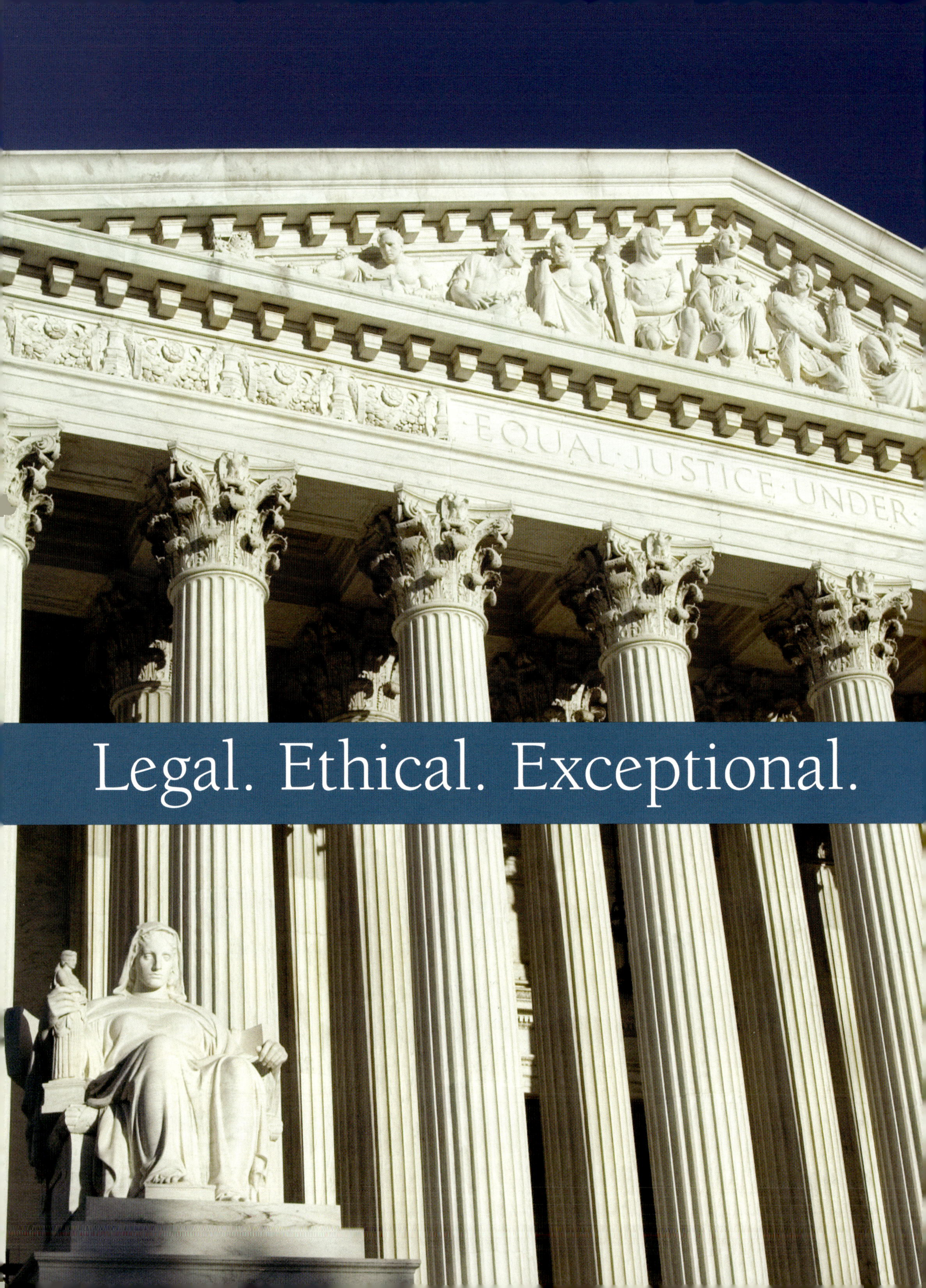
EQUAL·JUSTICE·UNDER·
Legal. Ethical. Exceptional.

MARGARET L. ACKERLEY
Senior Vice President and
General Counsel
World Wildlife Fund
Washington, DC

Those in the nonprofit community seeking inspiration for New Year's resolutions might take a look at the Senate Finance Committee's post-holiday lump of coal to the American Red Cross: its December 29, 2005, letter requesting an extensive array of information and documents relating to the Red Cross's board and governance structure and practices. It is a stark reminder that all of us in the nonprofit community, particularly board members with fiduciary obligations, need to act to ensure that our organizations operate legally, ethically, and with strong attention to what BoardSource terms "compliance with integrity."

Nonprofit directors and executives know their organizations must meet federal and state laws and regulations governing their activities. Compliance as a function must be addressed regardless of an organization's size. But compliance with integrity requires more effort. Exceptional boards seek to meet this standard by addressing not only the details of what is legally required but also by going further to ensure the organization's operations and undertakings are conducted in a truly ethical, open, and responsive manner. This is the foundation of strong organizations. Here are six key areas that a nonprofit should focus on as it lays that solid foundation.

Statement of values and standards

One visible sign of an exceptional organization is board adoption of a statement of ethical values and standards that is "given life" by the board's adherence to the principles and its actions to ensure they are known and referenced regularly by staff. The Make-A-Wish Foundation, whose mission is granting wishes for children facing life-threatening medical conditions, is a leader in this regard. Two years ago the national office in Phoenix, joined by 71 local chapters across the country, adopted a statement of values and code of ethics that is signed and acknowledged annually by all 1,500 board members of the national and local organizations, as well as by all staff members nationwide. The statement and code guide board members and staff in compliance with legal and regulatory requirements by affirming the importance of meeting all such obligations. But beyond that, they direct board members and staff to aspire to the highest ideals for openness, honesty, and integrity in all they do. As Bob Bigler, Make-A-Wish's national vice chairman and treasurer remarked, "It sets a true tone for the organization and what we are trying to achieve."

Risk management

Another hallmark of exceptional boards is the seriousness with which they view their obligation to be aware of risk and ensure it is properly managed. Boards can stay aware of current and foreseeable risks, in both program and operational activities, through regular reports from management. The process can be formalized: The Nature Conservancy, for example, on the advice of the governance advisory panel that it assembled in the wake of criticism of its activities, recently established a Conservation Projects and Practices subcommittee for board review of

certain activities. This subcommittee reviews activities that are of "first instance" or that present reputational risk to the organization. Boards can also obtain information from whistleblower hotlines, ensuring that reports of wrongdoing are shared promptly with the board. Less formally, board members can stay apprised of risk issues through visits to the organization's work sites and discussions with staff.

Internal controls and audits

Many boards designate an audit committee to pay specific attention to risk issues. In some organizations, the functions of the audit committee are interwoven with those of a finance or executive committee. But specifically designating a group of board members, particularly those with audit, accounting, or other relevant expertise, to address these issues elevates this function of the board both symbolically and in fact.

In addition to overseeing audits, an audit committee can ensure that there is a sound system of internal controls that allow for the identification of incorrect financial information and reporting of fraud. A separate audit committee may, however, be impractical for smaller nonprofits, a fact recognized by the state of California in its Nonprofit Integrity Act of 2004, which requires an audit committee for nonprofits doing business in the state but exempts organizations with gross revenues below $2 million.

Even boards without a separately designated audit committee should consider an external audit. An annual external audit helps ensure accountability and internal controls by providing an outside view of the organization and its functions. An external audit may be required by state regulators and donors, including the U.S. government, in certain instances. Small organizations without the means to pay for an external audit should inquire about pro bono help. Most accounting firms have some clients who do not pay.

Insurance and emergency plans

Thus identified, risks must be managed, including ensuring adequate insurance coverage. Board members should be covered by sound Directors' and Officers' (D&O) policies and should further ensure that the organization has the insurance it needs to cover employees, programmatic and operational activities, and property. This is not a static undertaking; on a regular basis, and whenever an organization makes a change in activities or location, insurance must be reviewed.

Staff responsibility for this function should be clearly established. Organizations are encouraged to seek the help of professional advisers in reviewing and selecting various policies, as coverage issues can be exceedingly complex. If the organization has overseas offices or activities, the complexity deepens considerably (see sidebar on Mercy Corps).

In addition to adequate insurance, board members should query management to make sure there are emergency preparedness plans for natural or other disasters and that these plans are reviewed regularly, revised as needed, and known and understood by staff.

Performance evaluations

Exceptional boards give particular care to the selection and evaluation of the chief executive and senior executives, determination and review of compensation, and succession planning. These cannot be cursory reviews; performance evaluations must be thorough, and compensation analyses should be made against relevant market standards that take into account the full measure of compensation, including additional insurance, pension contributions, and other benefits and perks not strictly limited to business use (e.g., vehicles, cell phones, and home Internet access). Boards ignore at their peril their obligations in this area: The recent, highly publicized case of the compensation of the president of American University (including his personal use of university resources) and the focus on chief executive compensation in the December Senate Finance Committee letter to the Red Cross underscore the importance of ensuring that compensation is not excessive.

Conflicts of interest

Finally, a touchstone of compliance with integrity is a strong conflict-of-interest policy for board and staff. Board members' duty of loyalty to their organization requires that they put the interests of the organization above any individual interests. Transactions with any director and/or his or her family members, or with any company in which a director has a direct or indirect interest, must be subject to the organization's conflict-of-interest policy. The policy should be reviewed and acknowledged in writing by board members when they first join an organization and annually thereafter. All potential conflicts must be disclosed and considered by the board or designated committee before any agreements are made or actions taken that might involve competing interests of the board member and the organization. Even if there is no actual conflict, board members should be mindful that even an appearance of conflict can erode the public confidence and trust on which every nonprofit ultimately depends. And this is the crux of what is meant by compliance with integrity — going beyond what is acceptable to reach for a higher standard.

Reprinted from Board Member®, *Volume 15, Number 1, January/February 2006.*

GOING THE EXTRA MILE

Mercy Corps works in the midst of the world's most difficult conflicts and disasters to provide emergency humanitarian relief. The organization learned firsthand the challenges of navigating insurance coverage when it sought to provide international workers with workers' compensation coverage. With strong support from its board, Mercy Corps went well beyond local and national requirements to ensure that its staff around the globe had adequate protection, demonstrating precisely the extra effort that is at the heart of "compliance with integrity."

Mercy Corps' international general liability policy included coverage known as foreign voluntary workers' compensation/employer's liability, which was intended to provide needed coverage for staff in foreign countries. But here's the problem: These international policies have a general "war risk" exclusion that denies coverage for injuries or deaths attributable to war. Given where their employees work, this exclusion was a gaping hole in the safety net Mercy Corps sought to provide. The organization even paid extra to remove the exclusion for some employees but could not get it removed by any carrier for all employees.

The situation became a bit less burdensome in late 2004, when Defense Base Act (DBA) insurance became available to nongovernmental organizations with cooperative agreements or grants from USAID or the Bureau of Populations, Refugees, and Migration (BPRM). DBA insurance did not address the entire issue, though, because it was available only for employees paid entirely by USAID or BPRM funds. Undeterred, Mercy Corps obtained an accidental death and dismemberment policy through a London insurer for local staff in foreign countries. The policy provided coverage for employees not paid exclusively with U.S. government funds who might be injured in otherwise excluded war situations.

Putting together the pieces of this coverage puzzle to address all employees around the globe took considerable time, effort, and ingenuity. It still requires ongoing assessments and adjustments to meet changing employment and coverage situations. Mercy Corps' persistence in providing for employees in this way speaks volumes about its commitment not only to compliance but also to meeting a higher standard of ethics and integrity in its operations.

7

Audit Rules

The American Competitiveness and Corporate Accountability Act of 2002, commonly known as the Sarbanes-Oxley Act, was signed into law on July 30, 2002. Passed in response to the corporate and accounting scandals of Enron, Tyco, and others of 2001 and 2002, the law's purpose is to rebuild public trust in America's corporate sector. The law requires that publicly traded companies adhere to significant new governance standards that broaden board members' roles in overseeing financial transactions and auditing procedures.

While nearly all of the provisions of the Act apply only to publicly traded corporations, the passage of the bill served as a wake-up call to the entire nonprofit community. Indeed, several state legislatures have already passed or are considering legislation containing elements of the Sarbanes-Oxley Act to be applied to nonprofit organizations. In many instances, nonprofit organizations have adopted policies and altered governance practices in response to the Act.

Nonprofit leaders should look carefully at the provisions of Sarbanes-Oxley, as well as their state laws, and determine whether their organizations ought to voluntarily adopt governance best practices, even if not mandated by law.

Finally, it is important to note that two provisions of Sarbanes-Oxley apply to all entities, including nonprofit organizations.

Main provisions of the Sarbanes-Oxley Act

With two notable exceptions, the Sarbanes-Oxley Act affects only American publicly traded companies and regulates what boards must do to ensure auditors' independence from their clients. The Act also creates and defines the role of the Public Company Accounting Oversight Board, an entity empowered to enforce standards for audits of public companies. The Act explains processes for electing competent audit committee members and for ensuring that adequate reporting procedures are in place. In addition, it calls for regulations, and closes most of the loopholes, for all enterprises — for-profit and nonprofit — relating to document destruction and whistleblower protection.

Independent and competent audit committee

Recommendations

While it is too onerous to demand that all nonprofit organizations undertake a full audit, the board is responsible for assessing the potential benefits and costs of an independent audit. Nonprofits that expend more than $500,000 of federal funds are required to conduct an annual audit. In addition, participating in the Combined Federal Campaign requires an audit at $100,000. Any other charitable organization with $1 million or more in total annual revenues (excluding houses of worship or other organizations that are exempt from filing Form 990) should have an audit conducted of their financial statements and consider attaching a copy to their Form 990 or 990-PF. Smaller charities with revenues of at least $250,000 should choose a review or at least have their financial statements compiled by a professional accountant. The boards of nonprofit organizations that forgo an audit should evaluate that decision periodically.

All nonprofit organizations that conduct outside audits, particularly medium to large organizations, should consider forming an audit committee and should separate the audit committee from the finance committee.

The audit committee should be composed of individuals who are not compensated for their service on this committee and do not have a financial interest in or any other conflict of interest with any entity doing business with the organization. Most nonprofit organizations have volunteer board members. Nonprofit organizations that do compensate board members should not compensate audit committee members for their additional service. In addition, all nonprofits should ensure that no members of staff, including the chief executive, serve on the audit committee, although it is reasonable to have the chief financial officer provide staff support to the audit committee. The chair of the audit committee should be a board member and it is reasonable to expect that the majority of the committee members are board members.

The audit committee should ensure that the auditing firm has the requisite skills and experience to carry out the auditing function for the organization and that its performance is carefully reviewed.

The audit committee should meet with the auditor, review the annual audit, and recommend its approval or modification to the full board. The full board should review the annual audit and the audit committee's report and recommendations. Ideally the full board would also desire to meet with the auditor before formally accepting or rejecting the audit.

At least one member of the audit committee should meet the criteria of financial expert and have adequate financial savvy to understand, analyze, and reasonably assess the financial statements of the organization and the competency of the auditing firm. This may be a nondirector advisory member where permitted by state law.

Orientation of board members should include financial literacy training.

To support the accounting field and help ensure that nonprofit boards have available financial expertise, professional accreditation and membership organizations of accountants should require CPAs to participate in a pro bono nonprofit board service program.

Responsibilities of auditors
Recommendations

Large nonprofits should consider rotating at least the lead and reviewing partners of the audit firm every five years.

Nonprofit organizations should be cautious when using their auditing firms to provide non-auditing services except for tax preparation, which should be approved in advance, while the firm is contracted to provide auditing services.

The audit committee should require each auditing firm to disclose to the committee all critical accounting policies and practices used within the organization as well as share with the committee any discussions with management about such policies and practices.

Certified financial statements
Recommendations

CEOs or CFOs, while they need not certify the financial statements of the organization, do need to fully understand such reports and make sure they are accurate and complete. Signing off provides formal assurance that both the CEO and the CFO have reviewed them carefully and stand by them.

The CEO and CFO should review the Form 990 or 990-PF before it is submitted to ensure that it is accurate, complete, and filed on time.

Regardless of whether the CEO and CFO certify the financial report, the board has the ultimate fiduciary responsibility for approving financial reports. Just as the financial and audit reports are reviewed and approved by the audit committee and the board, the Form 990 or 990-PF should also be reviewed and approved. At a time when the Form 990 and 990-PF are published on the Internet by third parties, it is more important than ever that directors be familiar with the contents of the organization's 990 each year.

Excerpted from the white paper, The Sarbanes Oxley Act and Implications for Nonprofit Organizations. *BoardSource and* INDEPENDENT SECTOR, *2003.*

Beyond Compliance

TRINITA LOGUE
President and CEO
Illinois Facilities Fund
Chicago, IL

The Illinois Facilities Fund (IFF) is a private nonprofit organization, established in 1990 by nonprofit and community leaders to meet the need for growth capital for nonprofits serving disadvantaged communities. The IFF's mission is to assist Illinois nonprofits through loans, facilities planning, and facilities development.

Board Member interviewed President and CEO Trinita Logue to gain insight into how the IFF board goes above and beyond the call of duty in fulfilling its oversight role.

Board Member: How does your organization fulfill the compulsory compliance requirements?

Logue: We're required to send various reports to federal and local government agencies. If reports are late, we'll be in default. So it's important for us to be on top of all financial requirements. We try to make our reporting and compliance function as routine as possible, including an annual review by our auditors.

In addition to the information we supply to be in compliance, I always add narrative to describe what the IFF has accomplished. This gives me a regular opportunity to "bring the numbers to life" and promote the great work we do.

Board Member: What are your expectations for financial literacy on the board?

Logue: Because the IFF is a financial institution, every member of the board is expected to understand financial reports, at a minimum. Financial literacy is essential because board members have to be able to articulate strategic issues and advise the organization.

Board Member: The IFF has a sizeable bank account. How does your board handle financial oversight?

Logue: Our operating budget is $6.5 million, and we have assets of more than $80 million. The board gets quarterly reports, and we do five-year financial forecasts that are reviewed and updated every year. Because the board doesn't have day-to-day oversight, board members know it's essential to hire the right people for key positions. In addition, my performance and compensation are reviewed annually, but it's more than just a performance evaluation. They give constructive feedback and they follow up on outstanding issues. The board also looks at issues surrounding employee satisfaction, turnover, and staff retention, and it is not afraid to face up to difficult issues and get involved, when necessary.

Board members and I are true partners. I always keep them informed about large expenditures. For example, we're investing heavily in technology now, and they are supportive because they understand that this investment will make the IFF more efficient and effective.

As for transparency, we tell new board members everything! And we ask them regularly, one-on-one, if there's anything else they'd like to know. We have a policy book that explains how policy is made. Policies emerge from lots of sources — board members can suggest policies, and I can, too.

Board Member: How do your written policies and procedures help set the tone for board behavior?

Logue: We have a Statement of Values. I think it's important to have such a document, but I don't believe it's what makes people do the right thing. You end up with a great board because of a combination of things. It's partly developing a culture where excellence is expected. For example, we have 100 percent attendance at board meetings. That doesn't happen by accident. You can't have an involved, engaged board if people don't show up. On our board, it's not acceptable to vote if you haven't heard the discussion. We talk to potential members to screen out those who aren't committed to this kind of involvement.

Board Member: Are there unwritten "good practices" that you've found helpful in difficult situations?

Logue: My job is to keep the board running smoothly. In fact, it's part of my written job description. I try to build rapport, keep the channels of communication open, and ask for help when I need it. I believe the only way to solve problems is to shine light on them and get them out in the open. That's part of transparency, too.

This may seem obvious, but one of the best practices to avoid difficult situations in the first place is to communicate constantly. I talk to the board's leadership core all the time, in weekly conversations with the chair and treasurer and in a weekly meeting with the chair.

The way we fill board seats is another good example. We often give the retiring board member the task of suggesting a potential replacement. This is especially important when we need to replace a particular skill or ability.

Board Member: I understand that the IFF recently restructured its board and went from 21 to 14 members. Why did you do that? How is it working?

Logue: We got rid of all the committees and shrank the board to a "committee of the whole." We had so many "silos" (committees of loan people, real estate people, marketing people) creating undercurrents that it was difficult to have good financial strategy sessions. So we hired a consultant (we chose one who would challenge us) who helped us define several options for improving board performance. I was somewhat surprised (and a little uncomfortable) when board members chose the most extreme option: disbanding the committees. But I was proud of them, too. They put personal interests aside and did what was best for the board and the organization. After my initial shock, I realized that we've always done radical things; why stop now?

We made this change recently, so it's too soon to tell how it's all going to work. But I think the consultant helped us see the potential of making the change. We weren't satisfied to stick with the status quo just because it "wasn't broken," as one board member said. We all wanted something outstanding and that required making a change — not in response to a disaster or a scandal, but just because it would make the board even better at what it does. That takes courage.

Board Member: Sounds like you have a culture of doing more than you have to do. Any other advice for our readers?

Logue: I wish I could offer a checklist of 10 tips to ensure a high-performing board. But, of course, it's never that simple. Rules and written policies and audits help with compliance, but the real key is the people and the culture of involvement and integrity they foster. And, of course, having the courage to fix something even if it's not broken.

Reprinted from Board Member®, *Volume 15, Number 1, January/February 2006.*

SUSTAINING RESOURCES [8]

Exceptional boards link bold visions and ambitious plans to financial support, expertise, and networks of influence.

DIMENSIONS

- **FINANCIAL PLANNING** Exceptional boards approve activities that can be realistically financed with existing or attainable revenue, and they ensure that the organization has the infrastructure and internal capacity it needs. They examine major income streams and expenses, strive for a portfolio of sustainable revenue sources, and look beyond the annual horizon.

- **FUNDRAISING** Exceptional boards help shape fundraising strategies and participate in fundraising activities. By opening doors, attending events, generating contributions, and making personally meaningful contributions, they ensure the success of the organization.

Turning Up the Volume

DAVID H. HOSLEY, PhD
President and General Manager
KVIE Public Television
Sacramento, CA

If you ever wanted to be on an exciting nonprofit board, try guiding a public television station through the biggest technological change in the history of the American media. And do it while you're also going through a huge generational shift that's seeing your core viewers fade away while the mercurial Baby Boomers become your primary target for viewership and support.

Amazingly, some nonprofit boards excel in turbulent times and find ways to provide the resources needed to meet increasing demands. How? They embrace change, constantly scan their environment, and plan, plan, plan. They keep their eyes on the vision and connect themselves and other community leaders to their organizations. They succeed by linking fundraising efforts to vision and planning.

KVIE has such a board. When faced with the task of funding the station's transition from analog to digital broadcasting, it turned a challenge into an opportunity to excel.

The big picture

To navigate its way through the digital revolution, KVIE made strategic planning a core part of its operations. When I came on board in 1998, the station had an obsolete plan and was losing money on operations. In 90 days, I surveyed stakeholder groups, did an environmental scan, and put in place a short-term plan that got the station started on the transition to digital broadcasting. We then got to work on a long-term plan by adapting planning models used in the private sector, recruiting board members who had expertise in planning and worked in technology firms that excelled in it, and using scenario planning to lay out alternative directions for board discussions.

We worked hard to establish annual goals that were relatively few in number, significant to the success of the station, and easy to quantify and track. Monthly reporting on viewership, membership, major gifts, and local program production became routine, as did evaluation of progress toward annual goals. In recent years, we have communicated all of this information to the board and staff through monthly dashboards that present on one page a set of "gauges" that indicate how we're doing. Twice a year, we formally examine our progress toward goals at board and staff meetings.

We then sought to challenge our assumptions. We spent a lot of time researching and understanding our customers, the viewers of our three broadcast outlets — KVIE Channel 6; KVIE II, a cable channel serving our county of license; and KVIE-DT, our new digital channel. We discovered people in Modesto, Stockton, Angels Camp, and Fair Play were a lot like Iowans in their television taste and less like our neighbors in San Francisco. We tracked an emerging audience interested in online content and pushed hard to exploit the newer media opportunities, such as weekly e-letters with program highlights, online membership and pledging, and an electronic store. At the same time, we "superserved" those who had been our core supporters for decades, making sure their favorite shows were always in the same time slot and creating e-letters just for NOVA fans and British-drama lovers.

KVIE developed a maverick reputation, one that got us into hot water with PBS from time to time. But the results were undeniable — record audiences and fundraising totals.

8

SOCIAL ENTREPRENEURSHIP

As the demands placed on the nonprofit sector increase, while resources do not, many nonprofits have stopped relying solely on donations from foundations, individuals, or the government. Instead they are taking a proactive approach to generating revenue. These organizations are conducting profitable enterprises that generate revenue while fulfilling their missions.

The staff leadership and board members of these organizations are social entrepreneurs — they balance the need to generate revenue with the organization's mission objectives. Social entrepreneurship can come in a variety of forms, including

* generating sustainable new resources to support the organization's mission,
* working with existing markets to generate revenue for nonprofits,
* securing unrestricted funding to allow greater flexibility,
* decreasing dependence on traditional funding sources to become more self-sufficient, and
* finding new ways to leverage existing assets.

Many nonprofits have found that successful ventures in social entrepreneurship can lead to improvements throughout their organizations. With a more efficient revenue in place, board members can spend less time on raising funds and more time focusing on the mission, programs, and services of their organizations.

However beneficial social entrepreneurship may be, an organization cannot enter an earned income strategy hastily. Many risks are involved with social entrepreneurship, and a poorly planned business venture could end up damaging a nonprofit's finances, operations, or reputation. The board must ensure that the nonprofit has done the appropriate research and business planning and has earned the commitment and support from everyone connected to the organization, that the planned business venture is indeed legal, and that board members fully understand the risks involved.

A nonprofit should be in good shape before experimenting with social entrepreneurship. It should have stable leadership, a solid financial position, a united staff and board, and a clear vision for the organization that includes sustainability objectives.

If your organization is considering adopting entrepreneurial strategies, ask yourself

* Is there a community need for the product or service?
* What is the earned income potential?
* What are the critical success factors associated with each product or service?
* What environmental forces will impact your ability to generate earned income?
* Who are your primary competitors and how do you rank against them?
* What is the size and direction of the market?
* What level of market share can you capture?
* Is the timing right?
* Do you have the right people and are you willing to give them the freedom, responsibility, and authority for success?
* Do you have enough staying power in terms of dollars, time, and energy?
* Do you understand the risks?

Adapted from Unlocking Profit Potential, *BoardSource and Community Wealth Ventures, Inc., 2002; and* Merging Mission and Money *by Jerr Boschee, BoardSource, 1998.*

Dialing for dollars

The digital revolution provided KVIE's board members with a challenge they hadn't expected and many of them didn't initially desire. In fewer than five years, the station had to buy $5 million worth of new equipment. The station hadn't had a capital campaign since the 1980s and didn't have that kind of money in the bank. Some board members hadn't even been advised of fundraising expectations when they were recruited. The major gifts staff comprised a former administrative assistant who devoted only half of her time to fund development. So we started from almost zero. With the help of our marketing staff, we crafted a case for a campaign and took it to the barely functioning development committee.

Fortunately, there were a several leaders on the board who embraced the vision and were willing to stake out new ground. At the next board meeting, the motion to do a feasibility study started with "We don't have a choice. We have to do it."

And they did, helped by a handful of staff members. About half of the board took leadership positions in the campaign. All of them participated by either identifying prospects and opening doors or in some cases making requests. We converted the CFO and HR offices into a room where we demonstrated high-definition television and described how it would enhance KVIE's ability to serve the region. Board members and I hosted lunches for prospects, sometimes twice in the same day! The result: In under five years, the station received more than $5 million in pledges — the most money KVIE had ever raised in a campaign. We purchased equipment for a new way of delivering content, but more important, our board came together to accomplish a crucial task. It now has solid leadership and a much better understanding of its role in sustaining the organization.

Serendipitously, the end of that campaign coincided with the beginning of a major public television initiative to increase leadership giving. The results of the Major Giving Initiative have been even better than our campaign for digital conversion. We have had double-digit jumps in each of the last three years in major gifts, going from $145,557 in 2004 to $427,471 in 2006. Board-related giving (personal gifts, corporate support, directed gifts from foundations, and door-opening that's led to contributions) is way up, too, reaching $230,000 this fiscal year. By creating individual plans for our board members that focus on their skills and abilities, we've helped them find their fundraising "sweet spots." And the connections they are making with community leaders are impacting more than the bottom line. They're also making KVIE a better community asset. Our programming now complements regional initiatives and reflects our diverse region.

Plugging into new revenue streams

One of the biggest challenges KVIE has faced is volatile revenue streams. We're seeing changes in everything from government support to swings in local and national economies. Organizations that excel at identifying multiple sources of income are nimble at anticipating change. Fiscal oversight for our board includes making sure there is a mix of revenues so as program sponsorship ebbs there will be a new source that closes the gap. For KVIE, that's leveraging our digital telecommunications spectrum, such as renting part of our signal to companies that want to send data streams, and increasing the number of people who join online or shop at the KVIE.org store. We also have put resources aside to incubate new streams that might have little or no return in the short term, such as posting segments of programs on YouTube and partnering with a startup to post short clips of video on a Web site sponsored by advertisers.

Complementing the new ways of making money is doing the old ones better. There is a tremendous upside for nonprofits that are able to step up to best practices in standard ways of generating support for their mission. For us, that includes a strong direct mail effort, having one of the best pledge-drive teams in the country, and increasing our government and foundation support. Using technology to become more efficient, investing more heavily in staff training, and becoming better at measuring performance and adjusting our work with the new insight are helping KVIE to grow despite an explosion in choices for people who want to watch video content.

Keeping them tuned in

A strong partnership between volunteer leaders and the professional managers of a nonprofit can make an organization take off. In many cases, this means the board members have to be willing to do more. I've served on boards that chose to not engage in conversations about strategic issues because they considered management competent.

For my own station, I've been nervous that board engagement will mean board involvement in operations, and I've sometimes been more interested in maintaining the separation than embracing board member ideas. But when I've been willing to bring the board closer to what we do — create and acquire content and extend viewing through outreach to the community — board members get more excited and more willing to raise the money necessary to do the work.

Each year at our board retreat, board members indicate what they plan to do in the next 12 months. They complete a form that covers the whole range of their contributions of expertise, connecting to the community, and financial support. And then the professional staff develops an individual plan with each of them. We want them to be close to what they're passionate about and share their enthusiasm with others. When the board members do their self-evaluations at the end of the fiscal year, we discover that most of them have done what they said they would do, and some have exceeded their plans impressively.

It's a crazy time to be in public media. The demand for resources is constantly increasing. KVIE is fortunate to have a board that provides the support, expertise, and influence necessary to meet that demand.

Reprinted from Board Member®, *Volume 16, Number 4, July/August 2007.*

Funding the Future

JENNIFER PROGA
Director
Investment Consulting,
Deutsche Bank Securities Inc.
Greenwich, CT

In our investment consulting practice, we work with many endowments of varying size and type, with most in the $10 million to $100 million asset range. The investment knowledge of board and investment committee members covers a broad spectrum — from very experienced investment professionals to those with deep experience in other, unrelated fields. Regardless of their level of investment expertise, it remains incumbent upon all board and committee members who have been given the responsibility to oversee a fund's investments to understand the objectives of the investment program and its components. Even though the actual investment management is delegated to an outside expert, the investment committee plays an essential role in setting guidelines and policies for the expert and later in monitoring the performance of the portfolio.

An endowment's spending policy, the manner in which the organization has formulaically agreed to disperse its assets, is inextricably linked to the manner in which its assets are invested — after all, a spending policy has no meaning without the funds to finance it. Understanding and respecting this relationship is key to sustaining an organization's resources over time. The board and investment committee members must develop a better understanding of this relationship, and execute their responsibilities by casting well-informed votes on the investment issues related to sustaining their resources.

Endowment investment basics

Understanding some basic concepts about the pool of funds is key.

Endowment: Funds or property donated to an institution, individual, or group as a source of income. One of the goals in investing an endowment is to preserve principal. In order to do that, most institutions set up an investment program that will be able to support the institution's spending by generating a high enough return, on average, to at least match spending plus inflation and investment fees.

Spending Policy: The method that the institution uses to calculate the amount (typically expressed as a percentage) of the endowment that will be used to support its programs or operations every year. Most institutions depend on their endowments to, at least in part, fund their ongoing operations. Therefore, the spending policy provides a consistent process to move funds from the endowment to operating funds on an ongoing basis.

Investment Policy Statement: The foundation of an investment strategy. It clearly defines the goals and objectives of the endowment, and it aligns those goals with the investment program.

The governing body most often charged with oversight of the institution's investment program is a dedicated investment committee. Its responsibilities can range from investing in a few mutual funds (for a small endowment) to oversight of a sophisticated, multiple manager structure that includes hedge funds and private limited partnerships. Regardless of the structure's complexity, it's important for the investment committee to keep certain principles in mind when structuring the investment program:

- Structure the program to support the institution's spending policy or goals. In some cases, the committee may have the luxury of working in a structure where spending is set based on investment return, but that is the rare exception. Even organizations with large endowments are dependent on the success of the investment program to maintain spending levels.

- Properly define and assess risk. When overseeing an investment program, historically (with the help of advisors), most committees have defined risk as the volatility of returns, or the standard deviation of returns. If your endowment supports a substantial percentage of your institution's ongoing operations, you may want to define risk differently — for example, you may want to ensure that you have adequate liquidity to fund your portion of the operating budget for three years, or for a market cycle, in order to be able to ride out a bear market. Regardless of how you specifically define risk for your endowment, as the fiduciary for the organization, you will want to act in accordance with the Uniform Prudent Investor Act, which expects investment committees to make prudent decisions and allows them to delegate operational investment decisions to qualified and supervised agents.

- Determine your risk profile as a committee. The risk profile for the investment program is a crucial determinant of that program. How the members of the committee feel about active versus passive investing, the aggressiveness of equity and fixed income investments, or investing in hedge funds can vary widely. As well as representing the institution's need, it's important for the investment program to represent the committee's thinking as a group — and for it to not be dominated by one or two of its "expert" members. The risk profile can be developed in meetings, but if members are reticent about expressing their views openly, it may be best done in survey form, with the committee viewing and evaluating aggregated results.

- Ensure that your assets are adequately diversified. A broadly diversified investment program typically carries lower risk — make sure that you evaluate the risk of your program versus the broader market and other alternative approaches periodically. In the course of performing an asset allocation study, limit investments in higher risk and less liquid asset classes.

- Monitor your fund's performance. It is important to always consistently follow fiduciary best practices through ongoing performance monitoring on the fund, and to make adjustments as required (e.g., manager terminations, searches, rebalancing) in accordance with the institution's investment policy.

Real-world lessons

The Case of the Investment Guru: It is in an organization's best interest to seek out experienced investment professionals for membership on its board or investment committee. Many university endowments are

fortunate to have esteemed investment professionals among their graduates who have a great interest in supporting the institution, both financially and with their expertise. This can have a downside, however. One prominent university, with over a billion dollar endowment, had several senior investment professionals on its investment committee for many years. While they did an excellent job of assisting the committee in preserving principal, one very-well-respected member of the group was also successful in persuading the group to defer investing in non-U.S. markets until well into the 1990s. Less experienced committee members were hesitant to raise questions about this policy, and how it meaningfully deviated from the policies of peers. This was unfortunate, as the organization missed some of the non-U.S. equity market's best performance.

Lesson: How could less experienced committee members have built a case for investing in international equities in opposition of the well-informed opinion of the "Investment Guru"? While it would have been difficult to compile compelling evidence to support the alternate case on their own, there are literally thousands of money managers or unbiased consultants that would be willing to come in and present the case to invest in their asset class and product. Committee members could use these free resources to educate themselves privately or in official committee meetings.

SELECTING AN INVESTMENT MANAGER

JOHN DIERKES
Client Advisor
Deutsche Bank
Alex. Brown
A Division of Deutsche
Bank Securities Inc.
Baltimore, MD

To start the search for an investment manager, ask for recommendations from people you consider to be successful investors, other similar organizations, and your lawyer, accountant, and banker. For clarification, a financial or investment advisor brings financial planning and investment expertise to help you select professional money managers who buy and sell stocks and bonds. Your committee's goal should be to find a manager who will understand your institution's particular investment position and goals. Below are issues and qualifications against which you can measure a potential manager for your institution's investments.

Investment managers should

* have clients similar to your organization and share three or more references
* understand your organization's business and financial position
* have sufficient resources, databases, and research to provide investment decision support
* provide educational and professional credentials to determine their level of financial expertise, with five or more years preferred
* personally commit to handling your account and not switch you to an inexperienced junior associate
* share examples of investment plans and monitoring reports he or she has prepared for other institutions
* provide a fee proposal (e.g., annual fees, commissions) with a full explanation
* supply information on any customer complaints or regulatory violations

IMPORTANT NOTICE: This document has been prepared for discussion purposes only, and does not constitute an offer or recommendation. It is based on information from sources believed to be reliable. No representation is made that it is accurate, complete, or fair. We have no obligation to update or amend the information provided herein. We do not render legal or tax advice, and this document should not be regarded as such.

Regularly airing the pros and cons of any investment position, particularly if it deviates significantly from peers, should be an objective of every investment committee.

The Case for Caution: Many endowments posted excellent performance in the late 1990s and felt that it was riskier to maintain a balanced and more conservative investment program than to let their growth stocks grow to become an ever-larger part of their investment portfolios. In this environment, one medium-sized endowment grew concerned about its fixed income investments as the long-time manager held a high-yield issue that moved swiftly from being troubled into bankruptcy. When considering what action to take, the treasurer (a nonvoting attendee at investment committee meetings) reminded the committee that the endowment financed a significant portion of the university's operating budget. The endowment had a relatively aggressive investment program, with a high percentage of its assets invested in growth equities. As a result of this discussion, the committee determined that its fixed income investments should be considered a "safety net." This meant that it would view its fixed income holdings as assets that could be used to fulfill the university's operating needs for at least three years should they need to ride out a bear market without being forced to sell depressed equity holdings to finance operations in that period. They determined the appropriate amount of assets and decided to invest these assets in a more conservative fixed income assignment.

Lesson: While it can be a difficult step to take, making capital preservation a priority can provide significant protection in difficult market environments — which typically follow robust markets. Ensuring that part of your fund is structured to protect principal, or provide a "safety net," is one option. Having and following a well-developed rebalancing policy, as part of your investment policy, that mandates rebalancing into poorer-performing asset classes from stronger-performing ones is another. Any time is a good time to consider and implement such policies.

Guidelines for the investment committee

As investment issues and options increase in complexity, so do the challenges confronting investment committee members. How can they successfully navigate their responsibilities in the face of these challenges? We offer the following recommendations as guidelines:

- Always maintain a healthy degree of skepticism when considering all investment advice. Avail yourself of an informed expert who holds an opposing view whenever considering adding a new asset class or adopting a new investment posture for your fund. And remember, the simple questions are often the best ones — don't be afraid to speak up!

- Make sure that you have a well-defined process for making decisions regarding your investment program and that those decisions are grounded in a good understanding of your institution's spending needs and policy.

- Invest the time to develop a thorough, best-practices Investment Policy Statement (IPS). You do not need to have an investment consultant on retainer to obtain assistance in developing your IPS — many firms are happy to work with institutions on an IPS on a project basis.

Following these guidelines will help ensure that committee members can direct an investment program that focuses on servicing the organization's needs. By defining program performance objectives with respect to how the assets will ultimately be used and be preserved in order to sustain the organization, an exceptional investment committee demonstrates that it is focused on the nonprofit's fiscal health.

Reprinted from Board Member®, *Volume 14, Number 5, October/November 2005.*

Putting Your Money Where Your Mouth Is

KIM KLEIN
Editor
Jossey-Bass
San Francisco, CA

Board member responsibilities can be explained in a number of ways. "Fiduciary responsibility" is perhaps the most common. "Fiduciary" comes from a Latin word *fiducia,* which means trust or stewardship. Basically, a board member is to care for the organization, act out of loyalty to its mission and goals, and obey the bylaws, as well as, of course, obey all laws governing nonprofits.

More simply put, board members set policy. They hire, support, and, sadly, sometimes fire the chief executive. They ensure the organization has the resources it needs — whether it's people, dollars, or reputation. Board members should set an example for the community that the organization serves. They should be the most committed volunteers, willing to give the time and the money necessary to make the organization viable.

But of all aspects of the job, there's one that seems to bedevil board members the most: raising money. Boards seem to realize that raising money is one of the most difficult parts of their jobs — and the one for which they are most ill-prepared. In the 2004 BoardSource Governance Index, 22 percent of surveyed board members said they were dissatisfied with their personal fundraising performance. Chief executives were even more unhappy with 57 percent admitting that they were dissatisfied with the boards' fundraising efforts. (Remember: These numbers refer to the respondents to the survey, not to all nonprofits.)

And it's even harder for board members to wrap their minds around fundraising when it begins at home — initiating fundraising with their own gift.

Why should each board member make a financial contribution?

Simply put, each board member must test the proposition that the organization is worth supporting. Is this a good group? Should people, foundations, or the government give this organization money? The only true test is for the board member to ask him- or herself, "Let's see if this is a good organization. Would I give it money?" The answer must be "yes." When a board member gives his or her own money, then he or she is in a position to say to others: "I have given. All the other board members have given. We are not asking you to do anything we haven't done. However, our combined giving is not enough to run the organization and I'd like to invite you to help also."

Why is it so hard for so many board members to start their charity in their own homes? Let's examine the objections to board member giving one by one.

Many board members feel that, because they give their time, they should not be called on to give their money.

"Time is money," they will say. However, time is NOT money. Time is our most precious nonrenewable resource. When a day is over, that time is gone and we can never get it back. Everyone has the same amount of time in a day, but people have vastly unequal amounts of money. You cannot pay your staff or buy your office supplies with time. Try going to the bank and telling them you'd like to make your mortgage payment by volunteering as a teller! On the other hand, money is a renewable resource. You spend it, and then you earn more. People are rarely nervous to ask someone for their time, but are often very reluctant to ask someone for their money. If a board member is assigned to call three people and tell them about a meeting on Wednesday night, he or she will most likely do it. If two people can come to the meeting and one can't, the board member does not take this personally and feel like a failure. However, if this same board member is assigned to ask these same three people for $500 each, he or she will probably be very uncomfortable without training in how to ask for money.

Some board members don't have any money.

We've all heard that objection. But this argument also holds no water. The difference between a person who has made a gift and one who has not is the difference between zero and one. Once I have given one penny, I am now a giver. Hopefully all our board members will give more than one cent, but achieving "100 percent giving" simply requires each person to make some kind of gift.

I discourage the practice of requiring each board member to give a certain amount. Let each one pick an amount that represents a significant gift for each one. For one person this may be $25, and for another $2,500. But when I look around the room at the other board members, I should feel confident that each person has given thoughtfully. I don't need to know what anyone else has given. The chair can announce, "We have 100 percent giving and it adds up to $3,500.32 and so we have another $500,000 to raise." Each board member individually, and all collectively, has set an example. "Join me in making a gift to this great organization. I know it very well, and believe me, it is a great place to put your charitable dollars."

"I wasn't told that giving money was part of the job."

I hear this lament from many board members — and it's the only one that, in my opinion, has any merit. Usually out of reluctance to broach the topic, or sometimes out of a lack of understanding on the part of those nominating new board members, board giving is not mentioned. To someone who agrees to come on the board and then learns of this requirement, there is an element of "bait and switch." Usually explaining what happened and explaining the logic of giving, as well as the fact that there is no minimum requirement for a gift, calms the person down. This information should be included in the recruitment process to avoid the sudden surprise and prepare new board members for what is expected of them.

Making sure every board member gives money is part of building a team of people who share responsibility. If some board members give and others don't, resentments will surface. Those who give may feel that their donation "buys" them out of some work or that their money entitles them to more power. Those who do not give may feel that they do all the work while the "givers" have all the power. When board members know that everyone is giving his or her best effort to fundraising according to their abilities, the board will function more smoothly.

Nonprofits boards are where the best-thinking, most loyal, and most committed people come together. Good board members are willing to set aside differences in order to fulfill a mission and accomplish goals. They demonstrate their willingness to themselves, each other, and their community in many ways. Giving money may be the easiest to see, the simplest to measure, and the most important for setting an example that others can follow.

Reprinted from Board Member®, *Volume 13, Number 8, December 2004.*

Going Above and Beyond

JANE MENTZINGER
Executive Director
Chicago Communities In Schools
Chicago, IL

Every Thursday afternoon, I am reminded that I work with an exceptional board of directors — one that understands that fiscal health is essential to our organization's impact. At four o'clock each week, I have a standing conference call with a rotating group of directors primarily to discuss fundraising, but also related topics including strategic planning, program evaluation, and board development. These calls are an important tool in our plan to expand our reach and intensify our impact.

Chicago Communities In Schools (CCIS) is a small organization with a wide reach poised for great growth. Our mission is to reposition existing community resources into school sites to help young people successfully learn, stay in school, and prepare for life. We build sustainable relationships between schools and community agencies that will benefit children for years to come. Last year, we connected social, emotional, and health services to more than 38,000 students in the Chicago public school system. Presently, we touch less than 10 percent of the students in a school system where 85 percent of the children come from low-income homes. Our approach to growth has been deliberate and collaborative.

How did we get here? A year and a half ago, CCIS began a strategic planning process. As soon as our vision for the next five years started to take form, the board recognized the need for a financial plan to support our new strategy. First, we projected the cost of our new plan for the next 10 years. We discovered that we would need to double the budget in five years and triple it in 10 years — an ambitious goal for a $1.2 million organization.

At the same time that we understood the need for significant funding growth to implement our strategic plan, we also recognized that we had been on a funding plateau for the last several years. The organization had been through a development audit the year before and the recommendations we received immediately came to mind. We were told that in order to stay at our current funding level, more of our board needed to be engaged in fundraising. With our new strategic plan and goals, this would be even more essential.

Less is not more

Like many organizations, CCIS had a small number of directors doing the heavy fundraising lifting. Less than a third of our board was actively involved in solicitations. The nominating and board development

8

committee wanted more active directors so they began by reviewing board responsibilities. They highlighted the fundraising expectations for all directors. From this, we developed a peer-to-peer accountability system. We asked our most active directors to follow up on prioritized targets with less-active directors. While we saw our desired outcome in an up-tick of action steps, there was an unforeseen result. The lead directors were seeing more of the day-to-day challenges in engaging the board in fundraising, and they wanted more information.

Last winter, these two movements — the strategic planning and board engagement processes — fortuitously met. The board was invigorated by the program goals of the strategic plan and motivated to meet the financial challenge. At the same time, some of the directors had been exposed to the day-to-day development work and the need for greater board involvement. These directors wanted to be at the table more, especially as we began to develop fundraising and business plans to support our new objectives.

Let's talk

That is how we came to our regular Thursday conference call. The board had committed to funding the strategic plan and wanted to be involved — and make sure others were involved. Initially created as a time for our committee chairs to check in, the calls were soon opened up to all interested directors. We base our weekly fundraising discussions on our three priorities: renewing existing funders, acquiring new funders for the current fiscal year, and cultivating relationships for future gifts. This structure helps the board and staff stay on the same page. We discuss details, so that the directors can track where we stand in regard to our current budget and big picture issues, and to ensure that we have the same long-term vision.

The calls also serve as a key accountability tool — for both the board and staff. The staff uses tracking tools to share what has been accomplished week to week. Knowing that we have such a regular reporting expectation is helpful in pushing things forward internally. Directors know that in addition to the staff, they are now answerable to other directors.

Spurred on by participation in the weekly calls, members of the nominating and board development committee decided to distribute a personalized checklist of responsibilities to each director semiannually. This checklist has objective expectations, including whether the director has made a gift, solicited his or her personal contacts, or set up or attended funder meetings. The hope is that this tool will keep directors focused on their commitments.

Now CCIS is entering our next organizational stage with a board of directors much more engaged in fundraising. When they approved our new strategic plan, the directors knew they were also taking on the task of raising the necessary funding. Thanks to the weekly calls, the board did not get intimidated — it got motivated. Our board's unprecedented involvement in, and ownership of, fundraising bodes well for the realization of our vision. Thanks to our board's commitment today, students will benefit for years to come.

Reprinted from Board Member®, *Volume 14, Number 5, October/November 2005.*

WHAT'S YOUR AGENDA?

CCIS's weekly conference call is a lot more than just a chance to chat. To make sure the call meets its objectives, covers all important issues, keeps everyone focused, and stays within the allotted time, an agenda such as the following is used.

1. Review fundraising priorities
    a. Renewal prospects
        i. Updates
        ii. Items needing action
    b. New prospects
        i. Updates
        ii. Items needing action
    c. Long-term prospects
        i. Review
2. Weekly meeting/site visits review
    a. Reports
    b. Upcoming
3. Other
    a. Strategic planning update
    b. Board development and nominating update
    c. Program update

RESULTS-ORIENTED [9]

Exceptional boards are results-oriented. They measure the organization's progress toward mission and evaluate the performance of major programs and services.

DIMENSIONS

- **METRICS** To gauge the organization's performance, overall efficiency, and ultimate impact, exceptional boards set clear expectations and define metrics for measuring progress. They integrate benchmarks against peers and calculate return on investment.

- **MONITOR** Exceptional boards monitor organizational performance by routinely reviewing financial and programmatic reports. They analyze quantitative and qualitative data and look for comparisons against plans, past performance, and peer organizations.

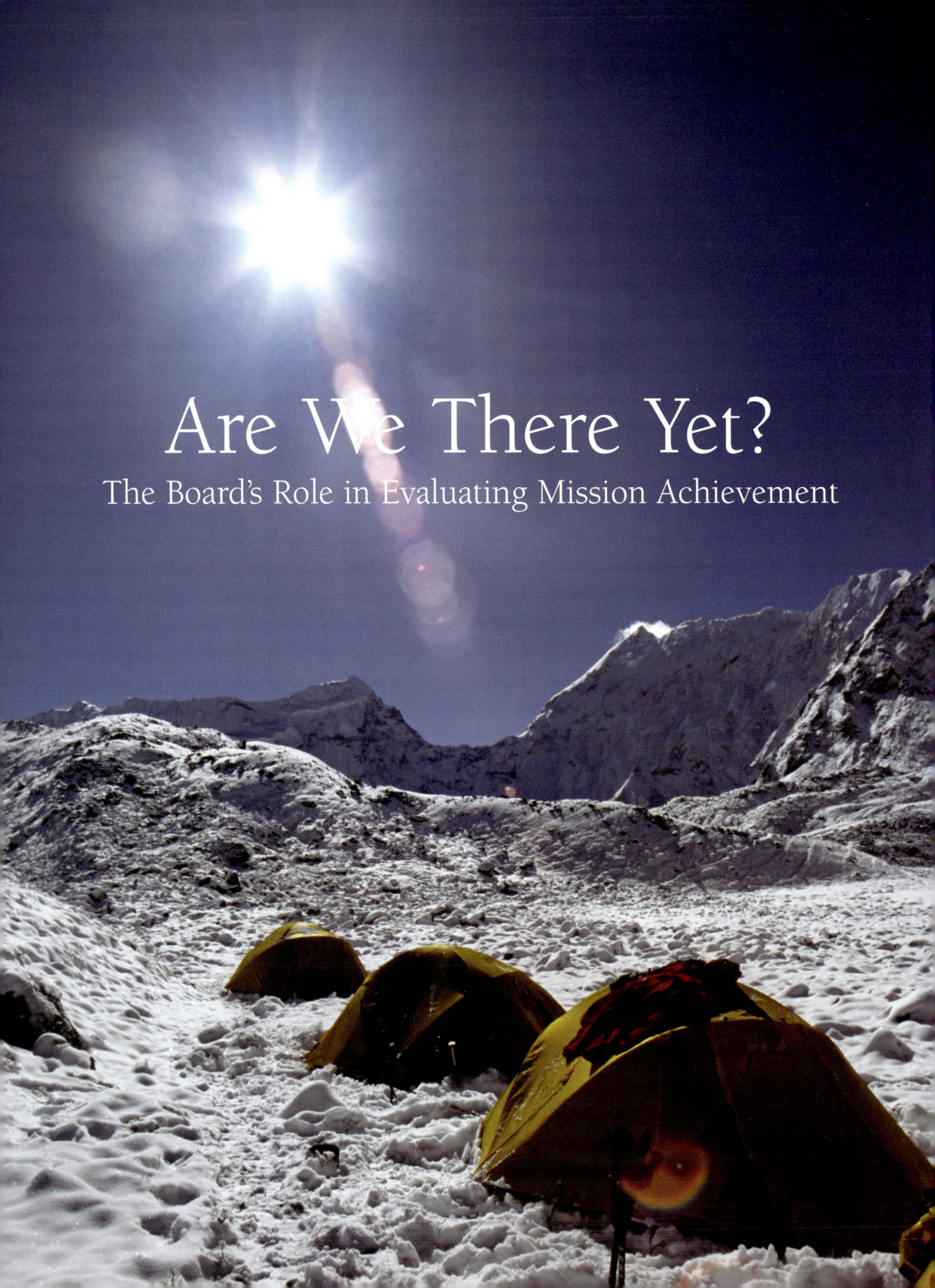

Are We There Yet?
The Board's Role in Evaluating Mission Achievement

PETER YORK
Vice President and Director
of Evaluation
TCC Group
Philadelphia, PA

The most important role a nonprofit board plays is mission steward. But what does this really mean? There are many elements to being good stewards and ensuring that the organization achieves its mission. First, the board must provide vision, inspiration, and direction, including making key decisions about how best to use organizational resources. Second, it must ensure progress by holding the organization and its leaders accountable for making the best use of these precious resources. Third, it must attract more resources by inspiring community, business, and government leaders to actively care about the mission. And fourth, it must evaluate mission success.

Few boards do an effective job of evaluating mission success (an enormous task) or measuring client satisfaction and resource use. To do these right, the board must demand and receive high-quality information to help it assess if and how the organization's programs (the tools to accomplish the mission) are meeting their goals.

Boards must learn more about the programs

Boards often view their role as setting direction and ensuring progress at the organizational level, focusing on the financial and operational leadership and management of the nonprofit. As a result, boards often leave program decisions to staff leaders, who will set program direction and ensure that programs achieve desired outcomes for people they serve. While the board should not get involved in day-to-day program decision making, it should understand if and how programs are successful. After all, the financial and operational functions of any nonprofit organization should be in service to the mission. Sustaining and strengthening the organization is not the end but rather the means to the end: mission success. The only way to determine mission success is through program evaluation.

Program evaluation is essential

Program evaluation is the formal process of measuring the quality of service delivery and the resulting outcomes. Typically, nonprofit organizations measure the amount of services delivered and sometimes the quality of that service. Few nonprofit organizations measure outcomes, e.g., improvements in client awareness, knowledge, attitude, motivation, skills, opportunities, and behavior. The board rarely receives evaluation findings, and almost never gets involved in developing and designing the evaluation effort.

When a nonprofit does conduct a program evaluation, it often does so because a funder has made it a requirement of program funding. Typically, when the funding ends, so does the evaluation. Using program evaluation as an accountability tool for funders is less likely to help nonprofits learn about what works, but rather helps the funder know whether its investment was worth it. Effective mission stewardship should be about accountability to the mission, not to the funders.

The board's role in program evaluation

The board, as the organizational leader, should insist on evaluation and require staff leaders to identify and set aside resources for conducting evaluation on an ongoing basis. It is the board's role to agree on expectations, allocate funds in the budget, and get and review information so that it can see how the organization is doing. That said, what does it look like when a board is appropriately involved? Let's look at the steps taken by the board of an organization that provides job training, placement, and coaching to homeless individuals.

Step One: Come to consensus on the assumptions for program success. The board met with staff leaders who led the process to come to consensus on the following assumptions: 1) the overall root cause of homelessness; 2) steps homeless clients would have to take to change their living situation; 3) the specific types and quality of job training, placement, and coaching services that would achieve the outcomes; and 4) the resources necessary for implementing services. The board and staff then drew a one-page picture of these assumptions in a flowchart format and labeled it their program model.

Step Two: Develop evaluation questions. Using their program model, staff leaders developed questions to help them determine if they were achieving mission. They presented these questions to the board, which provided feedback, asked questions not posed, and agreed on the final evaluation questions.

- Outcome questions: Did our clients get jobs? If so, did they stay in their jobs at least six months?
- Program quality questions: How much job training, placement, and coaching occurred? What was the quality of these services?
- Resource question: What resources were necessary to deliver services?

The board and staff also wanted to know the specific program practices that led to achieving the outcomes. This knowledge was important for making better decisions about resource allocation and for developing

---

TEN WAYS BOARDS CAN USE EVALUATION FINDINGS

1. Assessing the chief executive: Use program evaluation findings to hold the chief executive accountable for decreases or increases in client outcomes and program quality.
2. Fundraising: Use findings to inspire potential donors by telling and showing the mission story with facts and figures.
3. Recruiting board members: Share the organization's successes and challenges from a mission perspective in order to motivate individuals to bring their experience to bear in a way that is mission-focused.
4. Strategic planning: Use evaluation findings to assess the strengths and weaknesses of the organization's programs, identify opportunities and threats to the programs, and make resource acquisition and allocation decisions for mission success three to five years down the road.
5. Managing finances: Use findings about nonmonetary but essential resources (e.g., time, experience, expertise, facilities, equipment) to ensure that money is allocated for them.
6. Assessing the organization: Use findings about program success as a yardstick for assessing how well key organizational functions (e.g., knowledge management, program staff assessment and development, volunteer management, joint programming efforts with other nonprofits) support program delivery.
7. Celebrating success: Use findings to provide praise and recognition to staff.
8. Business planning: Use findings to develop replicable programs/services that could generate a fee-for-service revenue stream.
9. Managing human resources: Use program quality findings as a tool for providing more directed professional development and for conducting annual performance reviews.
10. Deciding to engage in a strategic alliance with other nonprofits: Use findings to identify resource needs for improving service delivery that could be addressed by collaborating or partnering with other nonprofit organizations.

"threshold" measures of the quantity and quality of service delivery that would signal that the organization might not achieve the mission. So, the following questions were also asked:

- What specific job training, placement, and coaching practices led to clients getting and keeping jobs?
- What specific resources were needed to support successful job training, placement, and coaching?

Step Three: Support staff leaders in the design and implementation of the evaluation. This organization chose to use an evaluation consultant because it did not have in-house evaluation expertise for things like research design, data collection tool development (e.g., surveys), or data analysis. Because the organization couldn't afford the consultant on a long-term basis, it asked the consultant to develop an evaluation system that the organization could continue to use on its own. The consultant also trained staff on how to analyze and present the data.

Step Four: Use the findings to make decisions for achieving mission. The staff reviewed the findings and shared key "mission-focused" results with the board. In this example, the board learned the following:

- Seventy-five percent of all clients were placed in jobs (short-term outcome).
- Sixty percent of those placed in jobs stayed at least six months (long-term outcome).
- Only 65 percent of all clients attended all of the training sessions (level of program delivery/quality).
- Some clients did not attend all of the training sessions because the organization was unable to provide bus tickets (lack of resources).

The evaluation findings also showed that when clients missed sessions, especially those pertaining to communicating with their managers about personal problems affecting their work, the clients were less likely to remain in their jobs for at least six months.

These findings allowed the staff, in close collaboration with the board, to make the following decisions: 1) the organization would provide bus tickets to clients, and 2) staff would pay special attention to attendance in the session on communicating with managers about personal problems affecting work.

The board used the findings and subsequent decisions to hold program leaders accountable for achieving better outcomes.

Four keys to evaluating mission

Boards that want to fulfill their stewardship role of evaluating mission achievement should adopt these four strategies:

1. Play a leadership role in evaluating mission achievement. Consider forming a subcommittee on program evaluation; work with organizational leaders to identify resources needed to design and implement an evaluation system; and hold the chief executive accountable for program outcomes.

2. Learn more about programs. Talk to program leaders and staff; observe programs in action; talk to clients; and get to know the constituency.

3. Make mission accountability a priority. Shift the board's primary focus from sustaining the organization to achieving mission; institutionalize evaluation as an ongoing process; and integrate evaluation and mission accountability into all organizational plans.

4. Participate in program evaluation activities. Taking direction from staff leaders, help determine what program success should look like; support staff leaders in developing evaluation questions and in designing and implementing the evaluation; and use findings to make decisions.

By living these strategies, boards will become better mission stewards because they will have better information with which to make leadership decisions, ensure progress, and attract more of the right kinds of resources.

Reprinted from Board Member®, *Volume 14, Number 6, December 2005.*

9

Evaluation: A Blend of Art and Science

Evaluation is a blend of art and science. It is a field relatively new to nonprofits but one that has been popular among businesses for years. A sampling of the techniques nonprofits are using to measure outcomes, most of which are not mutually exclusive, are presented below.

Dashboards

The notion of putting several outcome measurements onto a one- or two-page report was inspired by the dashboard of a car. Just as the car's instrument panel displays the key indicators a driver needs, an evaluation dashboard can sum up a large amount of information and display it in a concise, easy-to-read format. The dashboard technique is not an evaluation method itself. It is simply a way of displaying the results of an evaluation.

"You need to include, usually, a combination of numbers, graphics, and words in the mix," says Larry Butler, principal of The Ross Group in Boston, who has been using dashboards for years. "If it's all text, it wouldn't speak to all members of the board. People are unique in the way they receive and process information. Some people are better able to understand the numbers. Some need to see it graphically portrayed."

The dashboard is designed to be used on a regular basis — monthly, quarterly, or annually — whatever makes sense for the organization. Once it is designed, the same format should be used each time, from one meeting to the next, so board members can decode it quickly and spot changes, says Butler.

Consider the case of a hospital, he continues, "looking at patient satisfaction indices from quarter to quarter — opinions of food, nursing, and so forth. It may not be meaningful to have an isolated number. That may not tell you whether the score for your hospital is good or bad. You could compare it to other hospitals, but it's sometimes more useful to see how the score changes over time, just for your institution. Seeing the changes — either going up or going down — during the same quarter or the same period from year to year will tell you something. We're getting better at this or we're getting worse."

"When the elements of the evaluation appear together on one page, the human eye can take in a lot of information — particularly in the form of graphics — and see the connections and patterns much more readily than if they're separated on different pages," says Butler.

It's best to keep an eye on what is really important, says Butler, to be disciplined about sticking with measures that tie in with the mission. Even with carefully designed graphics, it is possible to swamp people with so much information that they lose the sense of connection with the big picture.

Sometimes when it makes sense to see more indicators on a regular basis, Butler suggests using a few key measures every time and alternating the others. "I've done dashboards where there are four windows of information, and two of them were the same from meeting to meeting, but the other two varied according to which meeting it was during the year. So that maybe we were looking at quality indicators annually but financial indicators every quarter."

Color is sometimes used to make an impact. It can help the eye pick up subtle differences, Butler says. But be selective, he cautions. "You don't want to overdo it. It is sometimes better to have just black and white or different shades of gray and reserve the color for highlighting something so it really jumps off the page. Use too many colors and it becomes rather bewildering."

Butler has seen the difference a good layout can make when presenting complex information to a board. "For me, the test is when an individual on a board feels emboldened to speak up on subjects he wouldn't have normally because now he understands them clearly. I remember once in an organization, one particular individual could always be counted on to say something about the human side of the organization — morale or human resources. All of a sudden, this guy started speaking up about finances because he saw we had been losing money on various programs for years.

"All that information had always been there, but it had never popped up graphically in a way that made it obvious. This guy suddenly became a finance expert based on the strength of this material." Butler adds, "This is all about empowering boards."

United Way of America's outcome measurement

In 1996, United Way of America developed an outcome measurement program that many United Way–funded organizations and other nonprofits have implemented.

It is an eight-step process used to evaluate nonprofit programs. It looks at resources used in the program (called inputs), analyzes how those resources are employed to further the mission (activities), and considers what products come from those activities (outputs). The final results are the outcomes.

For example, the inputs of a homeless shelter may include a building, money, staff, volunteers, food, and kitchen equipment. The activities would be feeding the hungry, providing shelter, and offering counseling. The outputs would be the number of people housed, amount of food distributed, and number of hours of counseling provided. The outcomes are the benefits: People are nourished and safe from the elements. Some may give up drugs or alcohol or even find permanent housing and jobs.

Many of the groups using this approach are social service organizations, but outcomes measurement can apply to other kinds of organizations as well, says Margaret Plantz, senior director, Outcome Measurement, United Way of America. "If you are able to identify a target audience, and you're trying to have some influence on their knowledge, attitudes, skills, behavior, position, or status, then outcome measurement is relevant to you.

Sometimes people ask if it's appropriate for arts organizations, or for cultural organizations, or religious organizations. When I get that question, I say to them, 'Can you identify a group that you're trying to influence and what influence you want to have?' If they say yes, that answers the question. They're trying to make a difference in how people see the world or behave in the world. They can identify outcomes."

Balanced scorecard

In both businesses and nonprofits, evaluations have typically analyzed financial data. The bottom line was simply, is the organization taking in more than it spends?

As businesses have grown more sophisticated, other methods have evolved that give a more comprehensive kind of evaluation. In the early 1990s, Robert S. Kaplan and David P. Norton wrote a book called *The Balanced Scorecard: Translating Strategy into Action.* The authors wrote about several pilot projects in which they conducted a balanced evaluation, which looked not just at the bottom line but also at how efficiently the organization was run, how much waste was generated, how satisfied customers were, and whether people were encouraged to suggest new ideas. The pilot sites included one nonprofit — the United Way of Southeastern New England.

At first, businesses picked up more quickly on the notion of a balanced scorecard, but recently nonprofits have started to show some interest. "The balanced scorecard asks you what the organization's strategy is and how you intend to fulfill it," says Harry Furukawa, associate director, Center for Quality and Productivity, University of Maryland. "The measures are an indication of that strategy. If you connect the dots between the measures, you should be able to determine the story of the organization's strategy."

One indicator in the balanced scorecard is waste, says Paul Arveson, director of the Balanced Scorecard Institute in Rockville, Maryland. "How much paper are people using? How easy is it to find things? How much time is being wasted? The scorecard helps you measure that." Comparing those amounts of time, he adds, motivates people to keep trying to do better.

Another indicator is learning and growth. When people have good ideas, do they have the freedom to develop those ideas? "That is the ultimate cause of improvement or growth in an organization," says Arveson.

The balanced scorecard does more than offer a comprehensive way of looking at an organization. It keeps the board looking forward. "The problem with looking at financial data is that it's a lagging indicator," he explains. "It tells you what happened in the past, but it doesn't predict what's going to happen in the future. That's what you really want to know. That's one of the reasons this is called balanced, because you're trying to balance the lagging indicators with the leading indicators."

SWOT analysis

A SWOT analysis is usually done during strategic planning. It stands for **strengths** (what are we good at?), **weaknesses** (what internal factors make it hard to do business, such as high staff turnover or an old computer system?), **opportunities** outside the organization (a new grant or congressional initiative), and **threats** (competition or anything else that could diminish or take away your business opportunities).

When organizations measure their outcomes, looking at the SWOT analysis can help ensure that everybody is on the same track. "You might have a wonderful board retreat to talk about strategic planning, and all these wonderful ideas get cooked up, but often the staff are back home providing services and going down another alley, leading to a misalignment of the organization," says Paul Andrew, national director of employment and community services at the Commission on Accreditation of Rehabilitation Facilities. "We try to get people to look at these outcome measurements, look at the goals your customers really want you to accomplish, then go back and look at your strategic planning, your SWOT analysis, and ask, 'Given these outcomes, what are the pertinent things that come to the top — things the chief executive and board should be working on to help staff achieve these outcomes?' That's managing your quality."

Logic modeling

Many nonprofits are chipping away at intractable problems. For them, measuring outcomes is a long-term process. But they need some kind of short-term measure to get a sense of how they are progressing — and to know if they need to adjust their programs along the way.

That is where logic modeling may come in. "Logic modeling is a useful tool in evaluations for a variety of reasons," says Mark Lelle, evaluation manager at the W.K. Kellogg Foundation. "One is that it allows you to do some evaluation in the short term for things that you typically aren't going to see the results of for several years."

Like the United Way's outcome measurement, the logic model looks at an institution's resources and the activities it engages in to move toward its goal. But it also considers assumptions that the organization makes along the way. Those assumptions may or may not ultimately prove to be true, but they are what the organization is going by. "It's called a logic model because it's a logical progression from your assumption to the resources you have to the activities that you plan to do to achieve your outcomes," says Lelle.

He gives the example of a long-term outcome to reduce death by stroke. "One of your assumptions is that sodium is somehow linked with high blood pressure, which is in turn linked with stroke. So a short-term outcome may not be reduction in death by stroke. It may be reducing salt intake. It allows you, then, in a short period of time to measure whether your program is on track. You haven't saved anybody's life yet, but you can see that there is some logical progression to the activities that you're doing — which may be an educational campaign to get people to decrease the amount of sodium they consume. You can measure whether that's had an impact. But you need to keep going because you may find at the end that even though you've reduced people's sodium levels, the incidence of stroke might not have gone down. So then you have to re-examine the whole logic model to figure out where the problem is."

The process can be complex, says Lelle, "but it's basically putting a mental picture on paper of what your programming is leading to and how it intends to tackle the problem.

"In the case of a social service organization trying to get people employed, long-term outcome is probably sustained employment. But because that might take awhile, they might measure increases in self-esteem in the short term. It might be that they have begun to apply for jobs — a necessary precondition to getting a job. So you come up with some logical progression of things that will ultimately lead to employment."

"It's an accountability tool," he says. "But it is also a good management tool. It's a way of clearly showing your staff or other people interested in the organization what you're about."

Reprinted from Board Member®, *Volume 10, Number 8, September 2001.*

This article was written by former Board Member® *editor John DiConsiglio. He is now a freelance writer. Larry Butler is now a senior consultant and strategic planning specialist with Maguire Associates. Harry Furukawa serves as vice president of learning and quality, Roger Schwarz & Associates. Mark Lelle is now an independent consultant.*

Measuring Success with a Pyramid

KATHLEEN WAGNER
Senior Vice President,
Conservation and Education
Philadelphia Zoo
Philadelphia, PA

The Measuring Mission story has its roots in 1997, when the Philadelphia Zoo board and staff invited community leaders, professional colleagues, scholars, and others to develop a new mission, vision, and shared values for the 123-year-old zoo. Their thinking produced a document called Vision 2020 that would shape strategy for the next two decades. The next chapter of the story began five years ago when the board of directors adopted a new strategic plan that re-affirmed the Zoo's mission and focused on goals to achieve national leadership in animal and plant care, wildlife conservation, and education. The board and staff envisioned an all-encompassing culture of conservation — in exhibits, programs and research, the guest experience, and outreach to the community. Launching the historic Zoo into a new century, the strategic plan emphasized the Zoo's commitment to conservation and education and its role as a community resource.

From vague to visual

Given the Zoo's mission statement ("to advance discovery, understanding, and stewardship of the natural world through compelling exhibition and interpretation of living animals and plants"), the board grappled with what "stewardship" really looked like in a zoo setting and how they could explain the role of conservation. Board members, experienced in business but largely unfamiliar with the world of conservation and zoos, charged the staff with distilling this lofty language and vague aspiration into an "elevator speech" that they could articulate to colleagues. The Zoo team refined its primary focus as "inspiring our guests to action and leadership in support of conservation." Good for a start, board members responded, but show us more. Staff then created a graphic model based partly on research in environmental education and partly on the Zoo's own thinking. The Mission Pyramid model articulates how programs and exhibits express the Zoo's mission. The model represents three levels of engagement and commitment in caring about and for the natural world; the Zoo demonstrates success by influencing its visitors to move up the pyramid. The ultimate goal is to inspire guests to become engaged in conservation and to demonstrate leadership in support of conservation.

Working through the mission committee (a standing board committee created to support the mission), the board of directors reviewed six different versions of the model over the course of eight months in 2002, and approved a final version in August of that year. Along the way, the board came back to the staff time

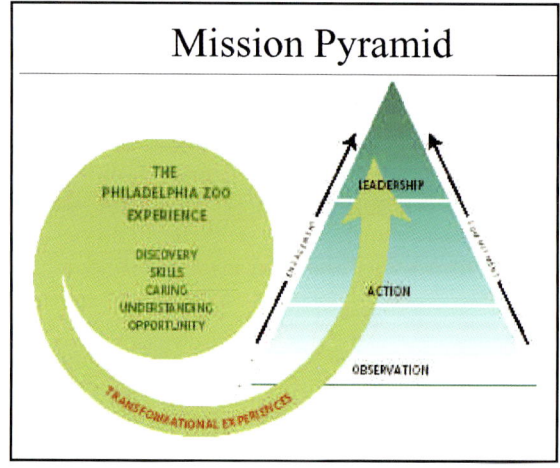

after time with questions and insightful observations. They probed: Would this model apply to all audiences? Would our scarce resources really allow us to influence people's conservation behaviors? What did "leadership" look like? And, most important, how would we know when we'd been successful? What sort of documentation would we expect to have?

The Mission Pyramid has been a useful tool for staff and board alike. Its sticking power was evident during the Zoo's 2003 re-accreditation visit when Board Chairman Peter Gould was asked about the Zoo's mission and he quoted chapter and verse from the Mission Pyramid! This simple graphic has become a rallying point and a filter for the staff and board to use when reviewing programs and activities.

Measuring success

Although the Mission Pyramid was thoroughly integrated into the Zoo's vocabulary, it was clear that the staff's work wasn't done. Challenged to find a way to measure return on investment, Zoo staff developed the Measuring Mission project with the goal of developing a long-term, systemic approach to measuring the Zoo's success in fulfilling its mission. Benchmarking and metrics were on everyone's mind; at one time the board mission committee even had a subcommittee called the metrics task force. But was this the right time? Could the small research staff tackle such a comprehensive project? Was the board ready to undertake a rigorous look at programs and exhibits, and was it ready to act on the results?

With the support of the mission committee, the board chair, and CEO Alexander Hoskins, the Measuring Mission project was launched with the goal of answering some critical questions.

- How does the Philadelphia Zoo influence its guests' conservation behavior?
- How do programs, exhibits, and outreach efforts encourage people to learn more, care more, and take action on behalf of the environment?

The Zoo launched Measuring Mission in January 2004 with a two-year grant from the Philadelphia Cultural Management Initiative, a program funded by the Pew Charitable Trust and administered by Drexel University. As part of the initial project, the Zoo team and its consultant, the TCC Group, developed a logic model that outlined a road map for the project, describing strategies, outputs, and short- and long-term outcomes. Key evaluation questions were derived from the logic model, and surveys and interviews were developed for three groups: visitors, members, and volunteers. Over the next two years, the team implemented the project with three different survey and interview instruments guided by a comprehensive evaluation plan. Periodically, staff and consultants reported results to a project steering committee of senior Zoo leadership and then to the board mission committee. Board support was evident throughout all stages of the project, and Chairman Gould invited staff to present results at a board retreat in spring 2005.

In the coming months, the board and staff will consider strategies to apply the findings. Of particular interest are findings that identify elements of Zoo exhibits and programs that relate to increases in commitment to conservation action. Equally important are established benchmarks that enable the Zoo to determine whether these elements are sufficient to provide the intended impact.

Challenges remain: The staff struggles to present technical data in a way that holds the interest of a busy board; board members look for actionable results and recommendations. A tight budget year means that resources are stretched and new grants are needed to fund the next phase of the project. But with encouragement from the board and CEO, and with a bit of luck in funding, phase II of the Measuring Mission project will launch in early 2006, with a second round of surveys and a national dissemination model planned.

Measuring success in fulfilling the Zoo's mission has been a challenge, but one that the board and Zoo leaders were ready for. The Zoo is passionate in its belief that the essential function of zoos is ultimately to preserve wild animals and wild places, primarily through public education, making it critical to determine how well we are accomplishing this.

Reprinted from Board Member®, *Volume 14, Number 6, December 2005.*

10

INTENTIONAL BOARD PRACTICES 10

10

CHARLES F. DAMBACH
President and CEO
Alliance for Peacebuilding
Washington, DC

The well-worn maxim that form follows function applies directly to effective nonprofit governance. Unfortunately, we're more inclined to structure our boards on a form-follows-form model. The form or structure that our organization has used for years — regardless of its effectiveness — tends to be accepted and applied for the present and the future.

Exceptional boards, on the other hand, carefully examine their function in the organization and create their form and structure to improve their effectiveness. If the primary function of the board is to provide expertise and perspective to guide the organization and set its direction and policies, why not structure the board's meetings and committees accordingly? BoardSource's book *The Source* identifies this governance principle as "intentional board practices." Instead of going with the flow of traditional structures and practices, exceptional boards intentionally build their governance structure and construct meeting agendas to meet the needs of the organization rather than follow a comfortable formula.

Create a structure that fosters creativity

An intentional practice approach to structures and meetings enables the board to better utilize the talents and resources of board members. Most nonprofit boards are comprised of community leaders and other people of exceptional knowledge and skill. Yet, few organizations take advantage of this remarkable resource. Committee structures impose mundane and needless tasks on busy people, and board meetings become tedious and repetitious exercises. The purpose of the organization gets lost in endless reports, while opportunities to enhance performance and produce meaningful results rarely make the agenda. The skill, talent, and resources of board members individually and collectively are wasted.

The board's fundamental fiduciary and oversight duties are essential, and they should never be shortchanged. Unless there is a crisis, however, the basic board tasks can usually be handled fairly quickly. Using consent agendas for routine business leaves time to tap into the creativity, wisdom, and talent of the board. Providing written reports in place of lengthy oral reports saves even more time. Periodic oral reports from each committee and from key staff are important, but they are not necessary at every meeting.

Exceptional boards move beyond structuring themselves just for basic oversight and fiduciary responsibilities. They create forms and systems that facilitate creativity and thoughtful engagement on the big issues that shape the organization. They develop meeting agendas based on the organization's mission, needs, and opportunities. They use techniques, such as generative thinking, to engage members so that meetings can become incubators of new ideas and concepts.

Select meaningful themes

My favorite technique for engaging the board in meaningful analysis is to select a theme for each meeting and allow ample time for in-depth analysis of that topic. For particularly important or complex issues, the theme can be repeated over the course of several meetings until the issue has been adequately addressed and the organization has developed appropriate policies, procedures, and programs.

Themes should be based on the particular needs or issues facing the organization. For example, a priority goal for the Alliance for

THE VALUE OF EXECUTIVE SESSIONS

Closed meetings, in-camera discussions, and executive sessions describe settings that allow the board to handle confidential matters behind closed doors without staff or outsiders present. These sessions may take place before, during, or after the normal board meeting. Appropriate topics include handling of personnel and client records, investigations on alleged improper conduct, chief executive performance assessments and compensation issues, business planning, financial discussions with an auditor, and legal negotiations. These issues need to be protected from open scrutiny and are not generally subject to public disclosure. There are also occasions when the board could benefit from an opportunity to share opinions candidly and openly among members. A regular session before the board meeting allows the chair to prep everyone for the coming discussions or simply let members express concerns. A session after the meeting provides an opportunity to address sensitive observations in private or simply offer a moment to "bond."

But there are rules that go with executive sessions:

* Address only predetermined issues; this is not a tool for avoiding a tough open debate or hiding behind closed doors.

* Communicate with the chief executive afterward to eliminate unnecessary secrecy and concern for being left out.

* Know your state laws and how they might deal with closed meetings if you are subject to the sunshine provisions.

Adapted from Meet Smarter by Outi Flynn. BoardSource, 2004.

Peacebuilding is to "build understanding of and support for peacebuilding policies and programs among leaders in government, business, media, philanthropy, religion, and other sectors of civil society." Therefore, we devoted half of a recent board meeting to communications with special emphasis on branding and shaping our message. We brought a terrific consultant to the meeting to help define the issues, guide the discussion, and offer expert advice. The board engaged in a lively and stimulating discussion, and, with the board and staff thinking and working together with the consultant, a whole new concept of communication strategies emerged. By intentionally engaging board members at this level, we made the best use of their brain power, and both board and staff achieved a better understanding of the issues and effective solutions. Of course, the staff will develop and implement the strategy, but the wisdom and special perspective of board members was invaluable.

There is virtually no end to the themes that can stimulate generative board engagement. An examination of national and local trends related to the organization can trigger meaningful analysis. A session on the board's own operations might lead to new policies about the size and composition of the board, revised committee structures, and identification of important new agenda items.

To make the best use of thematic sessions, background information should be presented in advance, and specialists and experts might be invited to provide insight and perspective. Adequate knowledge may reside within the board and staff, but usually not. A new and broader perspective from outside consultants, industry experts, and peer organizations can stimulate fresh dialogue and creative thinking.

Minimize standing committees

In addition to making board meetings more stimulating and meaningful with thematic sessions, exceptional boards apply the intentional practices concept to their overall structure — size and composition, permanent committees, and task forces. Boards that think about the best use of talent tend to minimize standing committees and use sharply focused task forces instead. Standing committees usually handle routine matters, and many of their tasks are redundant. The normal practice is a set of committees that mirror the staff structure. As a result, these committees tend to feel responsible for the productivity of the staff, which leads to interference and micromanagement. That is not the board's job; staff productivity is the responsibility of the chief executive.

Instead of having standing committees that mirror the staff structure, use task forces for program-related work and a standing committee structure that reflects the goals of the organization. For example, when board involvement is necessary to help develop or build a particular program or project, a special task force, rather than a standing committee, can be created just for that purpose. Once the task force completes its work, it should be thanked and disbanded.

Standing committees often seek reasons to exist and things to do that get in the way rather than add value. Task forces get the job done and allow members to move on to new challenges.

Standing committees focused on goals rather than staff functions can better guide policies and monitor overall progress. They can look into the future and identify needs and obstacles threatening progress. This approach takes advantage of the special role of board members as caring outside observers, organization overseers, and wise leaders.

Benefit from the brain power

Busy community leaders grow weary of board service when their only roles are listening to reports, approving budgets, and raising funds. Staff members grow impatient and frustrated when board members monitor them or tell them how to do their jobs. Neither approach provides an opportunity for the organization to benefit from the brain power represented on the board. By intentionally structuring meetings to engage the board in thorough analysis of important issues and structuring committees to focus on goals and results, board service becomes stimulating and enjoyable. This, in turn, helps a board add exceptional value to the organization.

Reprinted from Board Member®, *Volume 15, Number 6, November/December 2006.*

10

A Winning Number

DUANE A. BROWN
Vice President and General Counsel
American Diabetes Association
Alexandria, VA

What happened was this, the house began to pitch…. You probably know the lyrics from "The Wizard of Oz" song, which describes how I felt in 1998. That was when the volunteer and executive leadership of the American Diabetes Association (ADA) and its 50 state affiliates decided, courageously, to combine their resources and form one national organization. A number of major nonprofits have tried to accomplish this politically weighty feat, but many have stumbled.

Up to this point, each affiliate was run by strong and passionate local volunteer boards that believed very much in the mission of finding a cure for diabetes. The local volunteers, with input from ADA's national office, hired the state staff responsible for achieving financial and volunteer recruitment objectives. The affiliates benefited from the lay and scientific publications produced by the national office and, in consideration for a revenue-sharing agreement, could also use the logo and many trademark names associated with ADA's well-known signature fundraising events.

The politically savvy up-front and behind-the-scenes negotiations were arduous and lengthy. Many local volunteers were concerned with "losing their voice and influence" if the groups went "national" because a potential consolidation would require relinquishing all fiduciary responsibilities and independent authority. After nearly 18 months of fact finding, negotiation, and backslapping, all state affiliates were collapsed into one ADA. The 50 states were initially divided into 12 regions to give the volunteer leadership a continuing voice in the future of the ADA.

Consolidation has consequences

There were also unforeseen, more ominous, consequences of the consolidation: additional lay and professional representation on the ADA board of directors bringing the total to 56 members! Try to picture our board meetings: a very large room with reams of paper and two tiers of board members, including a 13-member executive committee (with three classes of principal officers).

Much like the way Dorothy's house dropped on the Wicked Witch of the East, board members suddenly realized in 2004 that the current arrangement was not terribly efficient or effective. Consequently, with absolutely no resistance from staff, the ADA board leadership took the bold initiative to downsize its ranks. It was clear from looking at several benchmarking studies that most corporations, nonprofit and otherwise, had reduced the size of their boards long ago. ADA's board decided that more constructive discussions surrounding issues like research expenditures, strategic planning, or creating new subsidiaries required a more intimate environment. In fact, because of the board's size, much of the work ordinarily reserved for it was being accomplished by the executive committee between meetings. Some board members found this disconcerting; downsizing meant board members would be closer to the action.

Thus, the Task Force on Effective Governance, which consisted of senior staff and board members, was assembled to look at who we were and what we were accomplishing — from a governance perspective — and to determine how to do more with less. The group broke up into subteams that drilled down and examined the work of traditional committees and councils. No one was really surprised by the findings. Many committees and councils no longer had the same purpose they did back in 1998. With the ADA's growth in revenue (from $125 million at the time of the merger to $220 million today) came a change in the scope and purpose of these entities, including the makeup of the voting membership and the professional composition of the board.

Reducing size through restructuring

One outcome of the task force's work was to consolidate several and eliminate many obsolete board structures. In fact, three major committees, 12 councils, and five project teams were eliminated. All committee and council charges and responsibilities were rewritten and updated, including the audit, finance, nominating, executive compensation, and executive committees. The volunteer structure was also re-organized to provide clearer avenues for input and upward mobility for both the lay and scientific communities. Because some board members complained that they felt removed from the nuts-and-bolts discussions (so much work was being done by the executive committee and passed to the board on the consent calendar), a fourth board meeting was added annually to focus solely on strategic planning. The ADA bylaws were modified to reflect many of these changes.

The most dramatic change was the decision to reduce the size of the board from 56 members to 31. How should this be accomplished since each member had a three-year staggered term? How could we tell an aspiring board member that there was no longer room at the table?

Taking it one step at a time

We approached this from two perspectives. First, we wouldn't try to downsize entirely in one year. Instead, we set 2009 as the goal to achieve our magic number of 31. Second, we changed the number of members we added as other members rotated off. Traditionally, 12 members were added to the board each year as terms expired; we reduced that number to six as 12 rolled off. There's talk of reducing the number by another 30 percent to 21 members when we achieve our first goal in 2009.

The recommendations were overwhelmingly adopted by the board because members could clearly see the benefits and efficiencies to be achieved by reducing board size. Each professional group that originally comprised the board will remain but will be smaller. While the process will be gradual, everyone can see Emerald City at the end of the yellow brick road. The ADA is currently looking at ways to continue to use the talent of those whose terms have expired, perhaps on one of our key task forces or teams looking at new business initiatives.

Will meetings be more effective? Will the character of the board change as a result? It's still too early to say, but give me a call when I get back to Kansas and I'll let you know.

Reprinted from Board Member®, *Volume 15, Number 6, November/December 2006.*

GROW OR SHRINK?

While the average nonprofit board size is 17 members, there's no one "right" size. Each board has to figure out how many members it needs to get the work done while still being efficient in its decision making. Think about the following advantages and disadvantages as you consider calibrating the size of your board to increase its utility and efficacy.

Large boards

* More workers to manage the load
* More perspectives to enrich discussion
* More help with fundraising
* Loss of individual accountability
* Challenging logistics

Small boards

* Easier communication and coordination
* More meaningful involvement
* Participation counts
* Potential burnout
* Limited viewpoints

Adapted from the topic paper, Size of the Board. *BoardSource, 2005.*

Finding Inspiration in Our Own Backyard

SUSAN SANOW
Deputy Executive Director for Programs
Center for Nonprofit Advancement
Washington, DC

Searching for and discovering "best practices" in the nonprofit community is easy in the Washington, D.C., area. The Washington Post Award for Excellence in Nonprofit Management is a 12-year-old competitive program that identifies outstanding examples of nonprofit management. Hundreds of organizations have competed, and hundreds of great ideas have been shared with the community as a result.

This article highlights some winning board management practices that the award committee has discovered over the years. Some ideas are simple and can be implemented quickly; others will take a major commitment by an organization's leadership.

Board members in waiting

The Community Ministry of Montgomery County (www.communityministrymd.org) has built a reputation as a strong program serving people in need in Montgomery County, Maryland. This reputation enables the organization to grow a list of candidates waiting to serve on its board. All of those waiting to serve get involved in the organization in some way — as mentors, volunteers, or financial donors. Their "waiting-to-serve" period often deepens their interest in the organization's work. The board and staff continue to intentionally reach out to individuals, knowing there may be a lapse in time between recruitment and actual service.

Individual board member assessments

While many boards embrace the idea of assessments, they are rare in smaller community-based nonprofits. But the board chair of N Street Village (www.nstreetvillage.org), a shelter for homeless women in Washington, D.C., introduced them at a time when the board was in a position to "step it up" as they emerged from a difficult period. The self-assessment, a tool designed to assess board performance and identify priorities for board activities, was non-threatening and confidential, so individuals felt they could say whatever was on their minds. The board chair took responsibility for the analysis and then shared the results with the entire board. The first assessment was successful and the board is now conducting a second one. The assessment helped the board

- develop a more professional work style
- define gaps in board talent
- cultivate and vet new members
- motivate and energize new members to "kick it up a notch"

Passing the board chair baton

NPower Greater D.C. Region (www.NPowergdcr.org) is a Washington, D.C., organization that provides technical support and services to other local nonprofits. It created a six-month handoff process between its incoming and outgoing board chairs to ensure a smooth transition. Because the outgoing board chair had served during a critical time of rebuilding, the board felt that the leadership changeover was particularly important. It wanted to make sure that the lessons learned and momentum gained during this time were not lost. The frank kickoff discussion, which included the executive director, addressed hopes, dreams, and concerns for the organization's future. The two chairs jointly planned the annual board retreat and agendas for the year's board meetings. As a result, the two board chairs developed rapport and were able to guide the leadership change. An unexpected benefit from the kickoff discussion was the board's newfound focus on its objectives and culture.

Keeping the board connected to mission

PHILLIPS Program (www.phillipsprograms.org), an Annandale, Virginia, school for the developmentally disabled, has figured out an interesting way to keep board members connected to mission and program: They must participate in an in-school activity and then report on it at the next board meeting. Some board members have attended the Thanksgiving dinner with students, while others have gone to graduation, participated in a staff meeting on a critical subject, or served as mentors. Overwhelmingly, trustees have reported that this participation reminds them of the real mission of PHILLIPS, increases their motivation and feelings of connectedness, and helps them make better board decisions.

Board exit interviews

After experiencing a wave of board resignations, Miriam's House (www.miriamshouse.org), a Washington, D.C., residential community for homeless women with HIV, implemented a policy of interviewing all exiting board members. The board chair, or an outside consultant, asked departing board members a set of questions, either by phone or e-mail. The answers were reviewed by the board chair and the executive director and then by the entire board. Several positive changes have come about because of the lessons learned in the five years the exit interviews have taken place. The board

- wrote a values statement
- developed a financial accountability chart
- modified how it recruits board members
- did a lot of soul-searching about what it means to be a board member of this organization
- became more nurturing of new board members
- added educational items to the board meeting agenda

Reprinted from Board Member®, *Volume 15, Number 6, November/December 2006.*

BOARD SELF-ASSESSMENT

Board self-assessments help board members improve their work through better understanding of their roles and responsibilities. Here are some practical tips:

* Get each board member's buy-in in order to make this a true group effort. Without consensus, the board simply won't participate.

* If this is the board's first self-assessment effort, explore how others have done it and what tools they have used. Board members should determine together which tool is acceptable and fine-tune it to address important issues.

* Adequate time should be devoted to planning to ensure that board members have time to complete the assessment. A date should be agreed upon for a board retreat to discuss the results.

* The board should ensure that final recommendations from the board retreat discussions will be implemented by creating follow-up procedures. Board members should be provided with possibilities for self-improvement and clarified duties and expectations.

Excerpted from The Nonprofit Policy Sampler, Second Edition, *by Barbara Lawrence and Outi Flynn. BoardSource, 2006.*

CONTINUOUS LEARNING II

Exceptional boards embrace the qualities of a continuous learning organization, evaluating their own performance and assessing the value they add to the organization.

DIMENSIONS

- **ORGANIZATION** Exceptional boards deepen their members' knowledge of the organization's programs, constituents, and context through formal orientation and ongoing board education that draw on internal and external resources. They embed learning opportunities into routine board work and activities outside the boardroom.

- **GOVERNANCE** Exceptional boards regularly upgrade their governance practices. They gather feedback on their collective productivity and contribution to the organization. They undertake periodic board assessments to evaluate their own performance and use the information to strengthen board structures and practices.

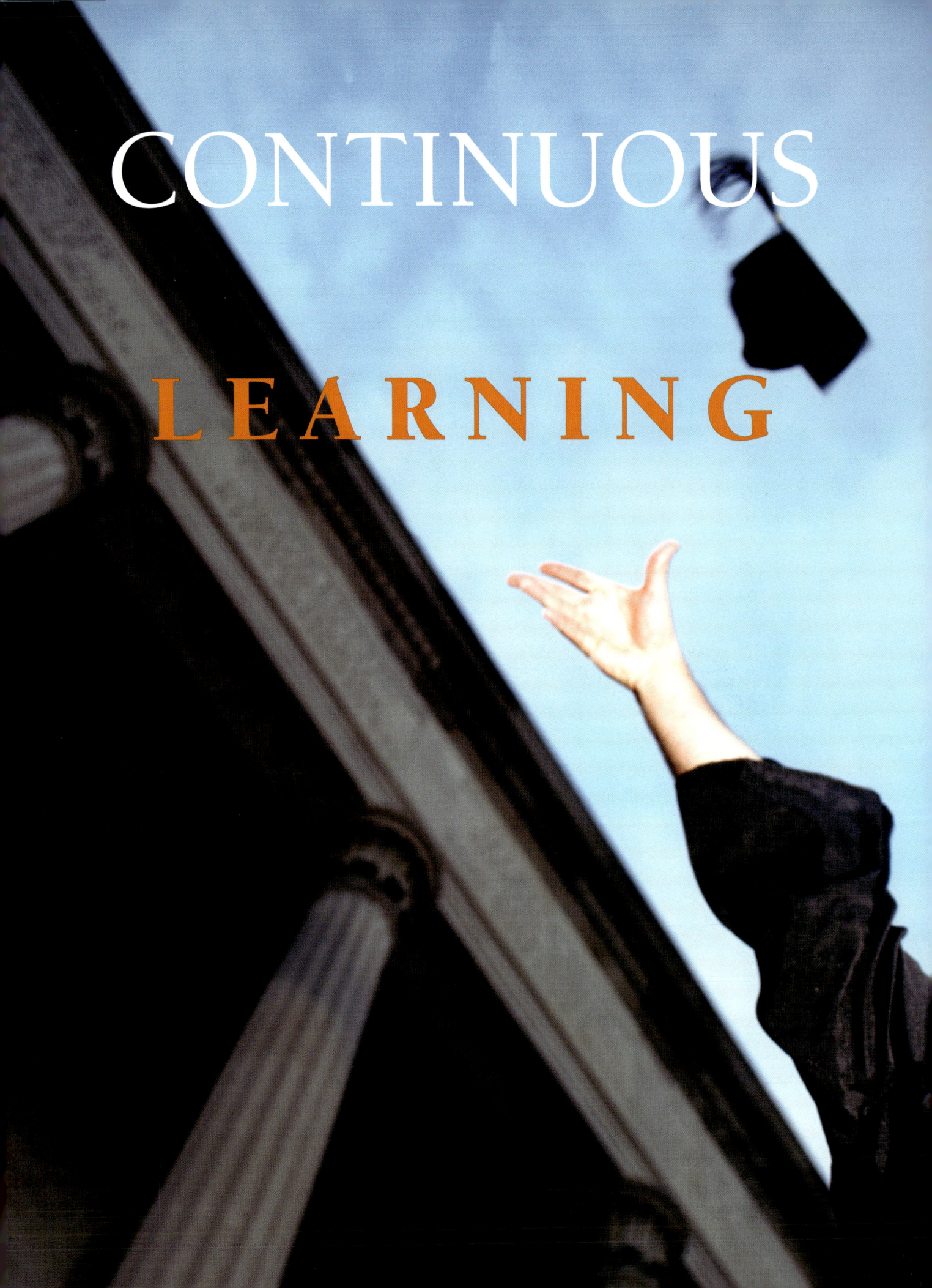

MELISSA DAVIS
Director, Governance
YMCA of the USA
Chicago, IL

Exceptional boards frame their work around proven practices — orientation, assessment, meeting planning, relationship building inside and outside the boardroom, and educational opportunities. They are confident that these practices can be customized, amended, updated, and refreshed in endless ways to meet constraints, opportunities, or lessons learned from them. But this framework of practices doesn't occur by accident; it happens by design.

The governance, or board development, committee generally is responsible for building and overseeing a formal framework, but the board chair–chief executive team set the tone and supervise the framework. It is essential to design a framework that infuses and supports the environment with attitudes and practices conducive to learning. The team can then watch for learning opportunities and incorporate appropriate "lessons" into the board's work.

For example, interviews with board members whose first terms on a national board were ending (a planned practice) revealed concern that two members had conflicts of interest that should have been disclosed. The governance committee worked with the organization's general counsel to design an educational session on conflicts of interest (an unplanned response) for the next board meeting that included case studies drawn from members of the board (with their permission) who had conflicts. Allocating precious board time and incorporating members' real situations reinforced a culture of shared accountability, respect, and openness (in an atmosphere conducive to learning).

Utilizing assets

Chait, Ryan, and Taylor point out in *Governance as Leadership* that an "organization profits far more from a knowledgeable board than from a loose federation of knowledgeable trustees." Boards conscientiously cultivate and recruit board members whose reputation and intellectual, political, and social capital promise great returns for the organization but then often fail to tap into these assets.

For example, a Girl Scout Council owned a camp where land use regulations had substantially increased the value of large tracts of land. It was not until developers approached the chief executive that the board recognized the need to assess the current market value of its land despite the fact that one of the region's premier realtors had been on its board for years. She stepped up and spearheaded the first appraisal in the board's memory.

Sharing board members' knowledge enhances and hastens learning and improves the chances that the "collective brainpower" of the board will enlighten the "collective mind" of the board. The simple inclusion of a "board roundtable" enables board members of a large environmental organization to share pertinent regional information and learn from one another. As board members deepen their knowledge of the organization, its industry, and its external environment, they are in a better position to help the organization advance toward its mission. The culture of continuous learning percolates throughout the organization.

Proven practices

The team creating the framework that will support continuous learning must engage in continuous learning itself. Structuring the board's work around proven practices, the framers test their assumptions, explore enlightened approaches, and agree upon methods. They guide a culture that nourishes learning — encouraging flexibility and variety,

SUGGESTED CONTENTS FOR BOARD OF DIRECTORS HANDBOOK

A. The board
 1. Board member names and contact information
 2. Board member bios, using standard format (not formal resumes)
 3. Board member terms
 4. Statement of board responsibilities
 5. Board member responsibilities
 6. Committee descriptions

B. Historical references for the organization
 1. Brief written history and/or fact sheet
 2. Articles of Incorporation
 3. IRS determination letter
 4. Listing of past board members

C. Bylaws

D. Strategic framework
 1. Mission, vision, and values statements
 2. Strategic framework or plan
 3. Current annual operating plan
 4. Programs list

E. Finance
 1. Prior year's annual report
 2. Prior year's audit report
 3. Chart outlining financial growth (sales, membership, programs, etc. — for the past five to 10 years)
 4. Current annual budget
 5. IRS Form 990
 6. Banking resolutions
 7. Policies related to investments, reserves, endowments, etc.
 8. Risk management policies

F. Policies pertaining to the board
 1. Policy on potential conflicts of interest
 2. Insurance coverage
 3. Legal liability policies
 4. Travel/meeting expense reimbursements
 5. Accreditation documents (if applicable)
 6. Whistleblower policy
 7. Others

G. Staff
 1. The chief executive's job description
 2. Staff listing (at least senior staff and those with whom the board might interact)
 3. Organization/team chart

H. Resource development
 1. Case statement
 2. Current funder list
 3. Sample grant proposal
 4. Sponsorship policy

I. Other information
 1. Annual calendar
 2. Programs list
 3. List of common acronyms and terms (with explanations)
 4. Current brochure(s)
 5. Web site information

J. Procedures to update board handbook

Excerpted from The Board Building Cycle, Second Edition, *by Berit M. Lakey. BoardSource, 2007.*

insisting upon time for generative discussion, resisting the status quo, and welcoming healthy tension. Then they pay attention to results, refining their methods or revisiting the whole design in light of lessons learned or shifts in the environment. No framework or practice is static. In a board culture conducive to learning, framers exercise innovative license but start with these tried-and-true practices.

Orientation. The board recognizes the importance of educating its painstakingly recruited members to the organization's particulars, often with a multilayered orientation that includes a group session supported by a manual, a tour of program sites and introductions to key staff, a knowledgeable mentor, and a personal conversation with the chief executive.

Boards with an emphasis on continuous learning understand that new members have needs and aspirations that led them to accept the position, and these boards incorporate interactive training and dialogue in their orientation as methods to ensure responsiveness to these needs.

Our own board development committee went back to the drawing board when a new chief executive, a redirected strategic planning process, and a change in board meeting date converged to reduce orientation time from one and one-half days to one and three-quarter hours! The committee saw an opportunity to experiment. They invested "face time" in getting acquainted and preparing new members for their first meeting. Then they scheduled three conference calls between the first and second quarterly meetings to focus new members on accessing the board Web site, understanding legal obligations, and comprehending financials. Finally, they increased both the amount and frequency of contact between mentors and new board members.

Assessment. The board acknowledges that evaluating the board's and individual members' work in an environment of trust and high expectation must happen continuously. Assessments can take on a variety of forms and may include gathering feedback on the board's collective productivity and individual members' contributions, analyzing results, and agreeing on improved structures and practices.

The YMCA of Greater Toronto adopted a comprehensive evaluation regimen that included a peer evaluation. Questionnaires were analyzed, summarized, and translated into an action plan by its governance committee for board consideration. In addition, the committee chair shared peer feedback with each member and developed individual action plans for the coming year. Members reported that the thorough process gave them a better understanding of roles, insight into leadership, and a greater appreciation of the value of their contribution.

Meetings. The board ensures that members' time together is spent productively focusing on what is most important to the organization. Agendas are created to allow sufficient time for "learning conversations" that expand board members' understanding, stimulate creative solutions, and enthuse board members. Meetings rely on consent agendas to handle routine items with one vote and dashboards to focus the board's attention on institutional performance, capacity, and condition. These practices respect members' time and intelligence and allow them to devote precious meeting time to more dynamic interaction.

Attention to simple details — such as congenial seating arrangements, incorporating icebreakers to learn more about members, and group work to design solutions — can reap remarkable returns. The board of the Lake Champlain Committee, a two-state environmental advocacy organization, literally gives members different perspectives by rotating meetings between New York and Vermont.

Relationship building and educational opportunities. Continuous learning occurs formally and intentionally in and out of board meetings. Reports from program staff or mini-lectures from local experts extend board members' knowledge and build relationships with significant members of the organization. Sending members to conferences upgrades governing skills, enlarges networks, and provides opportunities to share practices.

Learning continuously

Exceptional boards learn continuously by planning for learning and responding to learning opportunities. A 100-year-old family service organization held a legacy event to honor a founder of its long-running camp. Board members attended alongside past and present members, volunteers, and staff and listened to tales of a school bus (purchased with green stamps) that had once served as a boardroom! The legacy event achieved two results — it laid the groundwork for re-engaging former leadership in building an endowment and it generated a greater sense of responsibility and heritage in current board members. As a result, the board's governance committee is revisiting its plan of work. By designing for continuous learning, structurally and culturally, boards produce informed policymakers, advocates, and communicators who power organizations and strengthen communities. As one board member said, "My board has 'retrofitted' me to serve my community!"

Reprinted from Board Member®, *Volume 16, Number 1, January/February 2007.*

FOSTERING LEARNING OPPORTUNITIES

The board of the YMCA of Lincoln, Nebraska, found that committing several agendas a year to single topics increases participation and energy, paves the way for break-through ideas, and enables untapped leadership to surface. Thought-provoking questions, such as those below, are sent prior to meetings to stimulate out-of-the-box thinking and foster robust discussions and continuous learning.

Northwest YMCA (Fallbrook Development)

* What will be our stance if the school bond passes?
* Will we look to build immediately or master plan for the future?
* What type of commitment will be needed by Lincoln Public Schools?
* Is financing a building possible?
* Will a capital campaign be successful?
* Could the footprint be smaller with expansion space available once membership increases?
* How will building with the school maximize facility, YMCA mission, and community use?

Endowment — Foundation

* Should there be a policy to fund the foundation with excess operational funds if they exist?
* Should the planned awareness approach be more aggressive?
* What other communication steps should we take?
* How will this affect Strong Kids Campaign?
* How do we incorporate this program with future capital campaigns?

Downtown YMCA Improvements

* Recommendation has been made to keep our present location. Do you agree?
* Air conditioning is being studied. How important is this upgrade?
* What does our downtown presence mean to our mission?

Community Services Commitment

* Does the present commitment allow us to serve the underserved and still achieve association-wide needs and growth?
* What is our comfort level?
* Is the level of service realistic? Should it be higher? Lower?
* Grants are year to year. How do we mesh grant funding with stability?

Opportunities To Grow

JANET MURGUÍA
President and CEO
National Council of La Raza
Washington, DC

If there is one word to describe the last few years for our organization, the National Council of La Raza (NCLR), it would be change. Over the past three years, NCLR, the largest Hispanic civil rights and advocacy organization in the United States, has successfully navigated the most significant transition in its nearly 40 years of existence — thanks in large part to the strong leadership of a board committed to our mission of helping all Latino families. The board has been simultaneously respectful of our history and open to new ideas to help complete NCLR's transformation from a well-regarded Hispanic group into a powerful American institution.

A change in leadership

In 2003, NCLR's longtime president and CEO, Raul Yzaguirre, announced his intention to retire after 30 years. Knowing that his successor would have big shoes to fill and having witnessed rocky transitions at other nonprofits similar in mission and focus, the board took several important steps to ensure a successful and smooth transition. First, they made sure that the search process would be inclusive, transparent, and professional by engaging a leading nonprofit executive search firm. Second, recognizing the importance of having continuity in leadership and a base of institutional knowledge to assist the new leader, they extended the term of our then-board chair Jose Villarreal — a highly respected political and business leader in the Latino community — who otherwise would have rotated off the board. Villarreal had worked closely with NCLR's top leadership and his knowledge and experience provided a strong source of support for the new chief executive and the organization.

Our board and former president knew that successful transitions often were a result of having a new leader come from within the organization. Internal candidates are more familiar with the nuts and bolts of an organization and are often better known and viewed more favorably by staff and other stakeholders whose support is critical to any new chief executive. As a result, the board chose to create a new position, executive director and

chief operating officer, to enable the "heir apparent" to overlap with the last year of the outgoing leader's tenure. My selection, first as executive director and a year later as president and CEO, also demonstrated the board's reverence for the past and commitment to the future. I am the first woman and the first person of my generation to head NCLR. Monica Lozano, who was elected board chair when I was elevated to president and CEO, is also of my generation. She is the publisher of *La Opinion,* the largest Spanish-language daily newspaper in the United States and a nationally recognized business and community leader.

A change in approach

The chair and I persuaded the board of the need for a business plan approach to follow up on NCLR's strategic plan process. A business plan mentality would help NCLR be more thorough, transparent, accountable, and impact-driven than it had been in the past as it implemented its top two priorities.

First, NCLR set out to strengthen its relationship with its core constituency, the network of community-based organizations serving the Latino community in 41 states, the District of Columbia, and Puerto Rico, which make up NCLR's nearly 300 affiliates. Recognizing that we would benefit from external expertise, we engaged a consultant to help us. The board has provided guidance and input at every step in the way, including reaching out to affiliates with whom we'd had little or no recent contact. The business plan resulted in a new paradigm for the relationship between NCLR and its affiliates. Affiliates now have a more formal "partnership" with NCLR with clear and mutually agreed-upon criteria, goals, and expectations. There is also more accountability on both sides.

Second, the business plan called for the development and implementation of an integrated marketing and communications plan to help raise the visibility of NCLR's work and network of affiliates. Our research confirmed what we suspected: Though NCLR is a respected and well-regarded organization, it is not widely known. NCLR had never undertaken a communications effort before, and the board has provided substantial support, including setting up an ad hoc committee made up of members with communications and marketing backgrounds. The board has further lent support by adding new board members who are recognized experts in communicating with and marketing to the Latino community.

Respecting tradition

Throughout this period of change, several characteristics ensured continuity with our proud traditions. NCLR's bylaws require appropriate board representation of Latino subgroups, as well as geographic and gender diversity. In addition, one-third of our board is composed of affiliate representatives, while 63 percent of the board is made up of at-large members, both Hispanic and non-Hispanic, who typically represent key sectors of society. While some might see these bylaw requirements as cumbersome, they ensure that every time we propose a new priority or shift in direction, we do so with the backing of a board that reflects all of our major stakeholders. For example, in the process of redefining the relationship between NCLR and its core constituents, the affiliate representatives on the board had the unique capacity to assess the "value proposition" underlying the relationship from both perspectives. Similarly, in conducting research to help NCLR frame its "brand," it became clear that various Latino subgroups had different reactions to terminology; having a representative board ensures a thorough vetting of the trade-offs in selecting brand attributes and terms.

It's now the board's turn

After assisting the new chief executive and the organization with the transition from one generation of leadership to the next, the NCLR board decided to conduct a review of its own leadership and to discuss the transition it was making. Earlier this year, we engaged BoardSource to conduct a board self-assessment, evaluating the board's role in organizational monitoring, strategic thinking and planning, fiscal oversight, and fundraising. The assessment also examined the board's structure and makeup to see if it is compatible with NCLR's mission, work, and current and future needs. As a result of the assessment, the board will concentrate on three new priorities: fiduciary responsibilities, board governance, and resource development.

The board has been willing to engage in frank and honest discussions of its work and to contemplate change at the most fundamental levels while remaining stable and supportive through a time of considerable flux at NCLR. I can't overstate the importance of having strong, capable, and committed people in board leadership positions to ensure a successful transition. I relied heavily on the help and support offered by my two board chairs. I feel very strongly that it is a smart business practice to avail oneself of the counsel of former board chairs and members for their invaluable insights and knowledge of institutional history. As a result of ongoing knowledge-sharing and mutual support, NCLR and the board have completed a successful transition that can serve as a model for other nonprofit organizations.

Reprinted from Board Member®, *Volume 16, Number 1, January/February 2007.*

12

REVITALIZATION [12]

Exceptional boards energize themselves through planned turnover, thoughtful recruitment, and inclusiveness.

DIMENSIONS

- **COMPOSITION** Exceptional boards see the correlation between mission, strategy, and board composition and understand the importance of fresh perspectives and the risks of closed groups. They seek a diverse mix of expertise and experience among members, using tools, such as board profiles and term limits, to inform a continuous board member recruitment process.

- **LEADERSHIP** Exceptional boards recognize the importance of board leadership development and succession planning. They groom chairs and officers purposefully through a transparent and participatory process and experience smooth leadership transitions. With well-defined responsibilities, board officers and committee chairs set the tone for collaborative leadership and use their positions to strengthen the board as a whole.

Revitalizing
YOUR BOARD

12

JAMESON A. BAXTER
President
Baxter Associates, Inc.
Palatine, IL

Boards need their own source of renewable energy. Vital, effective boards understand this and are committed to the continual examination of their needs and composition. For the most part, boards charge a specific committee (usually the governance committee) with recruitment and orientation of new board members and with evaluation of all board members.

Although revitalizing the board through planned turnover, thoughtful recruitment, and inclusiveness is one of the biggest challenges a board faces, the rewards of introducing fresh perspectives and new energy are enormous. A board comprised of people with diverse perspectives and abilities, who engage in lively discussions to generate better solutions to problems, can offer its organization exceptional guidance and support. To help prepare for the process of revitalizing your board, consider the following.

Board structure

Basic structural decisions must be made by the governance committee with the concurrence of the full board. Decisions include board size, length and number of terms board members may serve, committee structure, and composition requirements. A hospital board, for example, might require that 25 percent of its members be physicians. An educational institution might require faculty or alumni/alumnae representation.

Board terms

In the distant past, board members served until they decided it was time to leave and often proudly reported terms of 25 years or more. Although debate still rages about term limits (see sidebar), most boards now set term limits and rules for renewing terms. I believe all boards should seriously consider term limits, both to ease recruitment efforts and to ensure new and fresh perspectives and thinking. If you are contemplating a change, your committee should thoughtfully consider how to manage a transition to a more defined structure. I was on one board where six founding board members drew straws to determine which two would retire in each of the following three years, thus keeping some, but not all, of these vital members on the board during the transition. On another board, as the transition was being completed, four long-serving board members retired at the same time taking 85 years of combined board experience with them! Although good, new board members had been brought on during the preceding years, it was nevertheless a startling moment.

Recruitment

No board function is more critical for long-term effectiveness than active, successful recruitment of new board members. Where this task might have begun in the past with recommendations of friends and colleagues, today it is a complex and substantive process that, although led by the governance committee, involves all board members. The committee first determines qualities that all board members should possess, such as commitment to the mission, basic financial literacy, understanding and respect for nonprofits, integrity, judgment, and, perhaps, some prior board experience. Most committees then

© 2007 BoardSource / Exceptional Board Practices: The Source in Action   129

use a structured approach to examine current board composition, creating charts showing not only professional and volunteer experience but diversity of gender, age, ethnicity, race, faith, and geography. The "holes" become obvious and are the starting criteria for the recruitment process. For example, a faith-based institution, such as a Catholic hospital that understands the power of diversity and the accompanying benefits of varied perspectives and experiences, may identify a lack of non-Catholic representation on its board and intentionally recruit to add this characteristic. Such a structured approach also encourages the board to think about the strategic direction it is setting, what the organization might look like in, say, 10 years and then to imagine the kinds of board members needed to support it. This process takes time and it can only happen if the current board is engaging in thoughtful and continuous recruitment.

Once the board has clearly defined its strategic membership needs, names of prospective board members who meet the selection criteria may come from several sources: current and former board members, the chief executive, and staff. The best of all outcomes is to have too many suggestions, which allows boards to develop a pipeline of prospective board members. This is essential because even interested candidates may have difficulty meeting your time horizons for joining the board due to their current obligations and schedules.

Orientation and mentoring

To become effective quickly, new board members need a detailed orientation program that includes meeting staff members, touring facilities, talking with committee and board chairs about how the board functions, and what is expected of members (including the possibility of making donations or attending various functions), reviewing the organization's strategy, and a thorough briefing on any legal issues, such as director liability or how intermediate sanctions impact the work of the board. I have seen voluminous briefing books that include minutes from prior meetings, bylaws, an organizational chart, the annual report, marketing materials, and various other financial information or analysis. The amount of information can seem daunting at first but will prove useful as time goes on.

Mentor programs can be particularly effective through the pairing of a seasoned and new board member. The two can get together outside the boardroom to talk about whatever is on the new board member's mind. Topics might range from how to interact with other board members, especially the chair, to clarification of items discussed in a committee or full board meeting. This process gives new board members an immediate connection and alleviates the feeling of being the outsider.

Leadership succession planning and ongoing evaluation

The governance committee has the task of continuous board improvement. This committee should, in conjunction with the board chair and the chief executive of the organization, determine the membership of the committees and ensure that there is leadership and training for the committees and the board. Board members should rotate committee assignments as part of a formal development program, ensuring increased knowledge, greater effectiveness, and fresh approaches to the work of the committee. It is important to have annual, formal processes for evaluating the board and its members. For board members, a good time to do this is when a term is concluding and renewal is being considered. Many boards have the executive committee do the evaluation to avoid the conflict that might arise if the governance committee evaluated people it recruited and oriented. The process begins with a written evaluation followed by a group discussion of the person. Ultimately, the mentor or committee chair gives feedback to the individual.

The discussion phase is particularly important because people bring a wide variety of perspectives to it. I participated in a discussion where the individual being discussed was particularly outspoken, often asking questions in a combative and critical manner that made other board members uncomfortable. In the review session, one person described him as a "flame-thrower" and, thus, not appropriate for the board. Another talked of his ethnic background and how that might explain and perhaps excuse his behavior and attitude. Yet another person saw the behavior as simply a matter of style and pointed out that other board members had styles that were also different and a bit "quirky." In the end, the person was asked to renew his term, and the mentor talked to him about adopting a more collegial style while retaining his ability to ask thought provoking questions. The committee agreed that every board can benefit from having a courageous person who will ask the tough questions and take unpopular positions in an effort to move the organization forward.

Why revitalize?

Constant renewal of a board is hard work. When you consider the natural tendency people have to stay in their comfort zone, where they know fellow board members and can predict how they will handle an issue, you can see how easy it is to develop a sense, albeit false, that your board will function better and more effectively in your current state. If you've dealt well with issues in the past, you are likely to believe you can carry that success forward. This comfort zone can lead you to resist necessary revitalization. The risk of not revitalizing, though, is a board that eventually becomes stagnant because it's denied new blood and the fresh and enriching perspectives that accompany it.

Revitalization and all that it requires must be enthusiastically embraced and undertaken with the belief that the organization will be stronger because of it. Boards with this understanding and well-developed culture quickly differentiate themselves from those that strive earnestly but fall short of full effectiveness. Revitalization is simply the non-negotiable and exciting element that powers exceptional boards.

Reprinted from Board Member®, *Volume 15, Number 4, July/August 2006.*

SHOULD YOUR BOARD HAVE TERM LIMITS?

A BoardSource survey revealed that nearly three-quarters of respondents have three-year board terms and those that limited terms had, on average, a maximum of two terms. Rotation can be a healthy and natural way to help a board grow with the organization and provide ongoing opportunities for renewal and revitalization. Here are some things to keep in mind as you ponder

Advantages of term limits
* Larger circle of involved volunteer leaders
* Balance of continuity and turnover
* Infusion of new ideas and perspectives
* Built-in rotation for ineffective board members

Disadvantages of term limits
* Loss of institutional memory
* Increased time for recruitment and orientation
* Need for continuous education and team building

Advantages of not having term limits
* Retention of passionate, active board members
* Deep understanding of organization
* Known personalities and group dynamics

Disadvantages of not having term limits
* High risk of organizational stagnation
* Fatigue, boredom, and loss of commitment
* Difficult to integrate the occasional new member
* Disconnect over time as environment changes

Adapted from the topic paper, Term Limits. *BoardSource, 2005*

Roles and Responsibilities of Board Officers

BARBARA LAWRENCE
Consultant
Somerset, NJ

OUTI FLYNN
BoardSource
Washington, DC

Board chair

The job of the board chair is one of the most challenging roles in the nonprofit world. A successful chair inspires a shared vision for the organization and its work, builds and nurtures future board leadership, and manages the work of the board. This position demands exceptional commitment to the organization, first-rate leadership qualities, and personal integrity. For many boards, success may rest heavily on the individual chosen to lead it.

Key elements

- As the chief volunteer officer, the board chair's duties run from managing the board to working closely with the chief executive. Additional duties may relate to his or her role as a spokesperson for the organization. If the board has an executive committee, the board chair also chairs this committee.

- In functioning as the team leader of the board, the board chair sets goals for the board, involves all board members in the work of the board (during meetings and through committee assignments), serves as the contact for all board members on board issues, and facilitates board meetings.

- In working closely with the chief executive, the board chair may be assigned responsibility for managing the overall board–chief executive relationship, such as developing meeting agendas and coordinating the executive's annual performance review.

Practical tips

- The chair's role is usually defined in the bylaws, but a separate job description should be created to outline the duties in more detail.

- The official title of the chief volunteer officer varies from organization to organization. The terms "chair" and "president" are the same, and the organization's bylaws should dictate which is used. The most common — and least confusing — title is that of "chair." This prevents confusion with the chief staff officer, who may have a title of president and chief executive officer.

- If the expectations for the board chair become too demanding and the position too time-consuming, it will be difficult to recruit new chairs. Often, some of the responsibilities and tasks can be shared with other board officers to make the position more reasonable for a volunteer.

Board officers

The most common board officers, beyond the chair, are vice chair, secretary, and treasurer. These positions are most frequently defined by state laws. The law may also indicate whether one individual can hold more than one officer position. In addition, some organizations have a chair-elect, which is one way to secure future leadership for the organization.

Specific officer duties may vary greatly from board to board. Particularly as the organization hires new and different staff, it is important to review and update officer job descriptions to reflect any changes in their focus.

Key elements

- Vice Chair: The office of vice chair provides the board with additional and substitute leadership. The vice chair generally fills in for the chair when the chair is absent and/or must leave the position permanently and without warning. The vice chair often takes on special projects, and some boards may divide various duties among two or more vice chairs.

- Chair-Elect: In some cases, a board may determine a candidate to succeed the board chair before the chair's term in office has concluded. The chair-elect may be given specific tasks, such as heading up the strategic planning task force. This position may provide a useful leadership development training ground and help to ensure a smoother transition when he or she assumes the role of board chair. In many professional associations, the chair-elect may be elected or appointed by the membership at large.

- Treasurer: The key volunteer financial management role in nonprofit organizations is the treasurer. The treasurer is responsible for overseeing financial operations to make certain that things are done in an appropriate fashion. In staffed organizations, the financial records are kept by the chief financial officer, controller, or accountant. In smaller organizations the treasurer may have hands-on responsibilities.

- Secretary: Depending upon the organization's size and staff, the job of recording minutes can fall to either a board member or a staff member. In the event that a staff member fills the position, the board's official secretary should review the minutes prior to distribution. In addition, the board secretary acts as the custodian of the board's records, although in most circumstances the board's important documents are kept in the organization's offices.

Practical tips

- As in the case for the chair, the primary roles for these officer positions are generally defined in the bylaws; however, consider creating separate job descriptions to describe the specific responsibilities of the officers.

- On some boards, the individual serving as vice chair may naturally assume the role of chair. In order for this assumption to be automatic, it must be defined that way in the board's policies.

- It is possible, and increasingly common, to combine the secretary and treasurer into one officer position. However, separate individuals should hold the chair and treasurer positions.

- Particularly for reasons of accountability and balance, and increasingly to meet the requirements of the nonprofit corporation laws of some states, consider appointing an audit committee to act as the main liaison to the outside auditor, electing someone other than the treasurer to serve as chair of the finance committee.

Excerpted from The Nonprofit Policy Sampler, Second Edition, *by Barbara Lawrence and Outi Flynn. BoardSource, 2006.*

12 The Board Member Shortage

Lisa Cain has looked in *The Washington Post* classified ads for everything from jobs to cars to apartments. So why not a seat on a nonprofit board?

That's how Cain found her way to the board of Calvary Women's Services, a Washington, D.C.-based nonprofit that provides housing and support services to homeless women. Cain, who is now the board president, is one of a handful of Calvary's 16 board members who were recruited through the classifieds. Some of the candidates who answered the ads have been terrific additions to the organization, she says. And some haven't worked out.

"OK, it's not exactly strategic planning," Cain concedes, noting that the board has since initiated more focused recruitment efforts. "But when you're searching for good board members, you'll look anywhere."

Newspaper ads. Professional contacts. That person you see each morning at Starbucks. Boards are scouring their personal and professional landscapes in search of new members. Perhaps no current issue vexes board members quite like recruitment. More and more, boards say they can't fill vacancies in an effective and speedy manner — not to mention find top board members who can bring needed skills and diversity to their organization.

According to a May 2002 Booz Allen Hamilton survey, boards are facing a dire recruitment scenario. Nearly 1.8 million board seats become available every year, adding to a backlog of 1.2 million standing openings, the survey notes. Minorities are particularly under represented on boards, accounting for only 14 percent of board members as compared with 27 percent of the population.

"There's no doubt that it's getting harder to find that top board member — by which I mean a person who brings the kind of resources you need to implement your mission," says Berit Lakey, BoardSource senior consultant. "Some people are concerned about the responsibility and liability that goes with being a board member. Some people simply lack the volunteer time. And, in some cases, particularly within small communities, there is a real competition for the people who have the skills and willingness to serve."

But even with so many factors weighing against them, experts say that boards can take advantage of a substantial pool of candidates — if they just know where to look.

"The good people are out there. They are willing and eager to serve on boards. They are just waiting to be asked," says Brooke Mahoney, executive director of the Volunteer Consulting Group, the founders of BoardNet USA, an online board member–matching service.

"I wouldn't say there is an absolute shortage of people willing to serve on boards. That doesn't mean it's easy to find them. What it really comes down to is hard work and time," says Mike Allison, director of consulting for CompassPoint Nonprofit Services. "It may take months. It may take years. But you can find good board members. What you can't do is expect a great board member to just show up on your doorstep."

New blood, new ideas

Too many boards aren't prepared to even begin a search process, Lakey notes. After relying on word-of-mouth as their sole recruitment tool, many boards haven't accepted recruitment as part of an ongoing board development plan. Many haven't fully assessed their board needs, profiling their board composition to find the specific skills and qualities they are lacking. Others are unprepared to change to better reflect their constituency.

"You sit at your board table and everyone around you looks like you," Lakey says. "And everyone they know looks like you, too. It's awfully hard to get new ideas, new perspectives, and new skills that way."

That's the exact problem that Calvary Women's Services faced. In addition to running newspaper ads, Calvary's greatest recruitment efforts came from word-of-mouth spread by fellow board members. But the board was dominated by 30-something white women, says Kris Thompson, Calvary's executive director. "We needed to get our board to look outside their intimate circle to bring in new blood and new diversity," Thompson says. "Our members would recommend their good friends. I'd have to gently tell them that this person matches their same skill sets, their same background, and their same contacts. Maybe she'd make a great board member. But she wasn't what we needed right now."

As Calvary has grown — the group is about to open its third shelter, ballooning its budget by a quarter of a million dollars to $800,000 — the organization has shifted its focus to its own version of "nontraditional" board members: older people who have greater board experience and are professionally and financially well established. "We're not looking for a whole board of old, rich, white men," Thompson says. "But we have to recognize that a lot of the people on our board haven't had experience in fundraising. Their personal giving is limited — and their access to people with funds is limited."

But identifying the right board members — those with both skills and resources as well as dedication and a passion for the mission — can be just as difficult when searching among experienced professionals. "The first person a

STEP BY STEP: RECRUITING BOARD MEMBERS

An organized recruitment process is vital to the ongoing health of a board. It helps fill vacancies and build a skillful and diverse board. If your board hasn't planned ahead, consider these recruitment steps as compiled by BoardSource consultants.

* **Make a board profile**
  Define your goals. Analyze your present board composition and look for areas where you need help. Do you need more people who are well connected with your constituents? Is your board diverse? Do you need extra fundraising capacity?

* **Form a governance committee**
  The search for board members should be ongoing. A governance committee focuses on this process on a regular basis. Its task is to find the best candidates, convince them of the benefits of board service, present the candidates to the full board, and, after the final nomination, make sure the new board members are well equipped to do the best possible job.

* **Have a search strategy**
  Governance committee members must constantly observe their environment and community to locate suitable candidates. They need to enhance the profile of the organization and make its mission known. They need to portray the board member's role objectively and accurately as well as lay out the challenges in positive terms.

* **Don't exclude your chief executive**
  The chief executive has the most intimate knowledge of the organization. She or he can assess the board's needs, identify valuable prospects, and help inform and integrate new board members into their new roles.

* **Cultivate a relationship**
  Finding new board members can be time-consuming. Decide first who is going to make the initial contact. The chair should follow up with a letter and appropriate material describing the organization. You can invite candidates to your special events like concerts or exhibits, a tour of the services, lunch with veteran board members, or even a board meeting.

* **Value orientation**
  All newly elected board members need a thorough orientation, no matter how extensive their previous board experience. Every board has its special characteristics, personal dynamics, requirements for involvement, and a structure that needs clarification. The governance committee should organize regular orientation for new board members.

nonprofit targets is the big CEO whose name they read in the newspaper," says Alice Korngold, president and CEO of Business Volunteers Unlimited, a Cleveland-based board development group that matches business executives with nonprofit boards. "You probably don't know anything about that person's expertise or background. They may not be the type of board member you really want."

In fact, many high-level CEOs are among the most disappointing board members, says Mary Tydings, managing director of Russell Reynolds Associates Inc., a search firm for corporate boards and CEOs. "Often you are looking for a big-name CEO who can open doors and write a big check," she says. "Even if you get them on your board, they may not do that for you. You'll often find far greater commitment and energy from that next level of business executive."

Thinking ahead

Often, the right board member match can still be found through focused recruiting by a board's governance committee. Expanding the role of a nominating committee, a governance committee embraces board orientation and continued training. It also identifies and cultivates quality candidates. "Think beyond Mr. Got Rocks and Madame Butterfly," says Carol Stone, president and CEO of the Volunteer Center of Orange County. "You know more people than you think. The person who runs the grocery store or the cleaners down the street. The secretary in your office building. These are people who have the time, the willingness, and probably more access and influence than you expect."

Others turn to search firms. But while large firms can cull from a vast pool of candidates, their fees can be prohibitive. Russell Reynolds's Tydings concedes that few nonprofits can afford their standard $75,000 search price tag, or even a more modest $30,000 fee. Smaller "boutique" firms charge fees of $5,000 to $10,000, "but they don't have nearly our resources," Tydings says.

Free services — like BoardNet USA or Business Volunteers Unlimited — have been successful for some nonprofits. Of its 1,500 online applicants, BoardNet says it knows of 43 candidates who joined boards and 23 boards that claim to have found members since the site launched early last year. Business Volunteers has placed 776 business executives on 241 boards in the last nine years, Korngold says. "It's very hard for a board to find the right candidates without vehicles like these," she says.

But third-party services don't replace the hard work and strategic planning each board needs, says CompassPoint's Allison. "It's not like ordering up a pizza," he says. "A lot of recruitment has to do with chemistry and nuance and cultivating long-term relationships."

Indeed, forming ties with potential board members can be time-consuming. Looking to add more diversity to its board, Calvary has asked one of its African American board members with ties to Ivy League alumni groups to help the organization make inroads to black business associations and student organizations. "We are paving the groundwork for the future," Cain says. "It hasn't paid off yet. But we're looking down the road. We are in this for the long haul."

Reprinted from Board Member®, *Volume 12, Number 1, February/March 2003.*

This article was written by former Board Member® *editor John DiConsiglio. He is now a freelance writer. Lisa Cain has completed her term as board president of Calvary Women's Services. Mike Allison and Alice Korngold are now independent consultants. Mary Tydings now leads a nonprofit practice for Russell Reynolds Associates. Carol Stone, now retired from the Volunteer Center of Orange County, is running Stone Nonprofit Consulting.*

Start Kidding Yourself

DONALD T. FLOYD
President and CEO
National 4-H Council
Chevy Chase, MD

NATALIE CHENG
Vice Chair
Board of Trustees
National 4-H Council
Chevy Chase, MD

During a meeting in 1991, members of National 4-H Council's board of trustees looked around the table and realized something was missing. We were working to improve 4-H, the largest youth development organization in America, and yet young people weren't represented on the board.

For more than a century, 4-H clubs have included young people in decision-making roles and given them "hands-on" learning experiences. Realizing these two key components of 4-H were missing within the board structure, the trustees knew they needed to invite young people to join.

Since then, as many as 10 young people between the ages of 12 and 22 have served as trustees each year. These young leaders have had great impact in moving 4-H forward. For example, during a revenue goal presentation, youth trustee Matt Cavedon spoke up and asserted that the goals were "not nearly aggressive enough," which caused us to increase them.

A partnership of equals

The youth trustees are given more than a voice and a ceremonial role. They have full voting power — their opinions weigh equally alongside those of adult board members. The youth trustees also serve on one of the five board committees.

The National 4-H Council board took youth input a step further when we decided to ask a youth to serve on the executive committee. For 11 years, a youth board member has filled one of the eight executive committee positions, currently as the vice chair for mission and performance.

Having young people who can contribute to the conversation as current 4-H members brings a fresh perspective and new ideas to the table. Sometimes they are so simple we wonder why the adults didn't come up with them.

Once, during a large stakeholder meeting, the group was having difficulty grasping the concepts. A youth trustee stepped on the podium and so clearly summarized the goals that the entire group immediately understood and embraced the strategy.

Having young people on the board reminds the adults of the purpose of the organization and provides a missing perspective. Youth trustee Matthew Ternus spoke up during a lengthy debate on programming to remind us, "Let's not forget, young people like to have fun." The comment caused the group to refocus the discussion. Another time, Andrew Dunckelman told the group it was making assumptions about youth and technology that were not correct. Without his insights, we could have made decisions about technology strategies that would have put us out of touch with our main audience, youth, for years.

Youth power in fundraising

Youth board members have joined in promoting the work of 4-H to corporations, too. Nancy Redd, a trustee since 2004, recently participated in meetings with the Toyota USA Foundation, New York Life, and NFL Charities.

Coincidentally, Redd had received a Toyota scholarship in college, so she took the initiative to bring along a poster featuring her as a scholarship winner. Her connections to the corporation and 4-H enhanced the conversations, and it didn't take long for Toyota to realize how strong an organization 4-H is for our young people.

Another board member, Nekeisha Randall, already had a relationship with Coke as a Coca-Cola, Inc. National Foundation Academic Scholar. Randall participated in a meeting of National 4-H Council and Coca-Cola Foundation executives who were evaluating 4-H for a grant and was able to clearly articulate the value of the potential relationship. Youth trustees can't be expected to serve the same fundraising role as the adults, in their personal donations or in leveraging professional relationships. But they are often the first to make contributions, and their checks of any size — coming from young people with no income — speak volumes about their commitment to the organization. In one case, the donation of a youth trustee far exceeded the adult board members: Redd donated half of her $50,000 earnings from an appearance on "Who Wants To Be a Millionaire!"

Challenges

Of course there are challenges to having young people on a board. One is the legal implications of giving minors a vote. National 4-H Council addresses that issue by including a requirement in our bylaws that stipulates that all board decisions made by vote must have a majority of trustees of legal age. We also make sure that the youth trustees do not constitute a majority of the members on each of the committees.

It sometimes takes a few meetings for the youth, who have been conditioned to not challenge adults, to be comfortable speaking their minds. They quickly learn that their voices matter, and they often speak more openly than adults. Once, an outside consultant made a presentation that completely misinterpreted the data. While the adults made mildly challenging comments, a youth trustee had the guts to tell the consultant that she was shocked at the report since it was contrary to everything we'd seen before.

School schedules can cause conflicts too. But both the young people on the board and their parents believe the long-term life benefits are worth the cost of missing some classes. Cori Byrum, a freshman at the College of William & Mary, quickly learned the need for time management. Going into her first year of college, she realized she needed to pay special attention to arranging her class work around the semiannual board meetings. The benefits of joining discussions at the national level have outweighed the logistical challenges involved.

A strong future

There is research to support the value we've found in sharing the board table with youth. A study about youth in the decision-making role found that adults who work with young people to make decisions about the organization report a higher level of commitment and energy around the room.

The study also showed that having a voice in the organization at a younger age encouraged the youth board members to support that organization for a longer time. Their involvement also made them more likely to use what they learned when working with other organizations.

National 4-H Council has been measurably strengthened by having youth on the board of trustees for the past 15 years. We've been forced to think more clearly about the role of youth in the organization and to be more inclusive. We've made changes to employment practices; for example, we now compensate our interns.

This experiment of including youth on our board — now a permanent and essential part of the 4-H culture — yielded benefits to both the youth and adult board members. The youth trustees provide a fresh perspective, challenge outdated processes, and bring everyone closer to the fundamental mission of 4-H — to empower youth to reach their full potential, working and learning in partnership with caring adults.

Reprinted from Board Member®, *Volume 15, Number 4, July/August 2006.*

WHAT'S IT LIKE TO BE THE KID ON THE BOARD?

Through my experience serving as a youth member of the National 4-H board of trustees, I have learned valuable lessons in leadership, public speaking, and teamwork. I have no doubt that this is a truly unique experience — a hands-on lesson that I could never have learned in school.

Of course, there were challenges when I first joined the board. Walking into a room of corporate executives and university presidents was extremely intimidating as I was just finishing high school. That feeling quickly faded, however, when I realized I shared a common focus with these adults.

I feel my input, and that of the other youth trustees, helps challenge board members to think innovatively, stay in step with the latest youth trends, and gain firsthand experience around the focus of 4-H's mission. As a 4-H trustee, I am able to take advantage of opportunities to help promote the organization that I wouldn't otherwise have.

I know this experience will have positive long-term effects in my life. I hope to use the skills I'm learning now in leadership roles in the future.

— Natalie Cheng